Pause
for
Thought
with FRANK TOPPING

Pause
for
Thought
with FRANK TOPPING

Including

LORD OF THE MORNING
LORD OF MY DAYS
LORD OF THE EVENING

Illustrations by Noeline Kelly

(L)

THE LUTTERWORTH PRESS
Cambridge

The Lutterworth Press
PO Box 60
Cambridge
CB1 2NT

British Library Cataloguing in Publication Data
Topping, Frank
  Pause for Thought with Frank Topping:
  including Lord of the morning,
  Lord of my days, Lord of the evening.
  1. Prayer-books
  I. Title
  242.8 BV245

  ISBN 0-7188-2524-1

Copyright Frank Topping 1977,1979,1980

This combined edition first published 1981
Reprinted 1986,1992

Printed in Great Britain by
St Edmondsbury Press Ltd, Bury St Edmunds, Suffolk

LORD
of the
morning

JOY

In this morning hour
I want a fresh chance
To start again.
I don't want to waste the minutes and hours
That have been given to me.
I want to be alive
To every experience,
In conversation,
In the mundane tasks of this day.
In moments of relaxation
I want to find joy in living.
Lord of the morning, help me.

Lord, help me to enjoy
The common things of my everyday life.
I often find myself saying that
Nothing happened today,
When in fact the ordinary events of my life
Make a rich pattern,

But they are so familiar
I hardly notice them,
Things like cups of tea and coffee
And meals shared with friends and colleagues;
Or listening to favourite family stories
That we have heard and told so often.
Lord of life, help me
To recognize the joy of simple things.
There are so many familiar mileposts
That I stop and lean on, every day,
So familiar,
That I don't realize how much
I enjoy their comfort and support;
Like the smile of the woman
Behind the shop counter,
The therapy of being lost
In a good book,
Or a radio play,
Or my favourite music.
The days are rich in pleasing moments
That I take for granted.
Lord of life, help me to realize
The joy of living.

When I come to the end of this day,
Help me to remember
The big problems that turned out
To be little ones,
And the things I worried about
That never happened.
Lord of laughter and joy

Help me to see,
To experience
And to treasure
Every good moment.
Lord of the morning,
Lord of life,
Lord of light, help me.

A NEW BEGINNING

Lord of the morning
I'm trying to forgive myself
For the mistakes I've made.
There are too many 'if onlys' in my life.
If only I had been more thoughtful,
If only I had been kinder.
I blame myself for so many things
Yet I cannot turn back the clock.
I have to live today,
Even with my self-inflicted wounds.
Lord, help me to live with myself.

Lord, in this hour
I need to be able to forgive myself
But I also need to be able to forgive others,
To *really* forgive.
How often have I gone through the motions of
    forgiveness,
Only to let my mind dwell on the wrong
    remembered?
And even to talk about the people who have failed
    me,
That is not forgiveness.
I know that I cannot erase experiences from my
    mind,
But even bitter wounds heal
And though the scars remain
They can grow faint and be forgotten.
Lord of life,
Help me to forgive, and to be forgiven.

It would be so good to be able to start again,
With a clean sheet;
To make a new beginning,
To be born again.
I want the old, muddled, muddied me to die.
I want new life.
Here am I, sinner and sinned against.
Is there a love that will cancel my sins?
Have I the love that will cancel
The pain caused by friends?
I know that it is possible,
I know that love can bring the dying back to life.
Lord, fill me with the love that you offer,
So that I may know that I am forgiven
And be so full of your love
That it will spill over into the lives
Of all the people I live and work with.
Lord of life, help me.

In this hour, Lord
Help me to look forward
Rather than to sigh over past events.
Help me to see the good that *can* be done
The caring that *can* be offered
The love that can be given.
Whilst I mope about myself
There are people waiting for the kindness I can give.
Lord, help me to give, to share,
To start again a renewed life.
Lord of the morning,
Forgive me and help me to start again.

PANIC!

Lord of the morning
I don't know why
But I sometimes feel a panic
Rising inside me.
I know it is irrational
Yet some days I am afraid.
The letter that falls on the doormat,
The sudden ringing of the telephone
Fills me with fear.
I'd like to escape, to run away
But there's nowhere to run
Except to you.

Lord of life
Why do I anticipate the worst
When time and time again
The worst never happens?
Even when it does, life goes on
And every day comes to an end.
Lord help me to overcome my fears
In this brief moment of reflection
Calm my mind
Help me to relax
Let your comforting Spirit
Enter into me
And fill me with peace.

In this hour
Open my eyes to all the things
That you have given
That help, support and lift
Troubled minds.
Let me find joy
In the beauty of a single flower,
A branch of a tree,
Or the vast embracing sky.
Help me to hear the love
That lies in the ordinary words
Of friends and family,
To remember the words of
Guidance that wait for me
In the rarely opened Bible or prayer book.
I know your love will lift me up.
Help me to trust you.

Lord help me to be thankful
That yesterday's problems have passed.
Help me to measure today
Not by the difficulties I *might* meet
But by the good things the day will bring.
Help me to know that *this* day
Will be full of gifts.
Give me the knowledge that no matter what
    happens
Today, or any day,
Nothing can separate me
From you and your love.
Lord of the morning, help me.

PURPOSE

In this morning light
The same old questions fill my mind
Like, what am I doing with my life?
What do I really believe in?
Is there a purpose for man, for me?
Lord I believe, help my unbelief.

In this morning light
I look for meaning.
What is it I want out of life?
What do I hope for?
What can I achieve?
What should I be doing with the days, the years
That have been given to me?
I want to be useful.
I want to be needed.
I want to love and be loved.
Lord of the morning, help me.

Lord of the morning
I find it so hard
To see what things really matter,
To see what is important in my life.
There are so many distractions,
So many demands,
Responsibilities, worries –
There is just so much to cope with.
And I do worry
Even though I know I am worrying
About the wrong things.

Lord of the morning
Give me this day
The wisdom to recognize what things are important
And what things are not.
Show me what to do
With the time and the talents you have given me.
Give me faith, give me hope,
Help me to trust in your guidance
All the days of my life.
Lord of the morning, help me.

OTHER PEOPLE'S PROBLEMS

In this hour
The world clamours for my attention
And I don't want to hear.
I don't like listening to the news
Or reading the newspapers,
They depress me somehow.
I suppose I don't really want to hear about
Other people's problems, yet
I know I cannot ignore my neighbours.
Lord of life, help me.

Lord, why am I afraid
Of being involved in the world around me?
I know the answer really:
It's because I cannot face
The demands that come
From so many who need help;
The poor who need my money,
The sorrowing who need my comfort,
The lonely who need my time.

Lord of life, give me the strength
To listen to the needs of others,
To give what I can, whether it's help or time.

Lord of life
The world about me is changing –
Different needs in different places.
I hear myself saying,
'How different things are from when I was young.'
Things are different, I am different,
Older, if not much wiser.
But you never change,
From age to age your love continues,
Your love is constant.
I know this
Yet I give and love so little.
Lord of love, help me.

Lord
Forgive me for ignoring the needs of others
And for missing opportunities of giving and serving.
If I see the truth, dimly,
If I stumble as a beginner in faith,
If I am, only now, beginning to wake up
To the fact of your love,
Help me, help me to see you,
To love you and to follow you,
Lord of the morning,
Help me.

BEING ALONE

In this morning hour
I am alone
With millions throughout the world who are alone.
Some are solitary in a kitchen
Or a bed-sitting room.
Others are in cars in traffic queues,
Or in the cab of a lorry on a road.
Sometimes it is good to be alone,
But loneliness hurts.
Lord of life, help me.

Lord of life
This loneliness is a passing thing.
Soon I will be with others,
Companions, friends, family,
And I can hide from myself
In their company.

But there is a deep aloneness
That is hard to live with
When the soul seems empty.
Lord of life, fill my emptiness.

Lord, loneliness comes in many forms.
For some it is the emptiness of bereavement,
Widow, widower or orphan,
Divorced or separated by circumstance.
Lord, you know what it is to be alone, to feel
    deserted.
Help me not to wallow in self-pity,
Fill my emptiness with your spirit
Until the cold core within me
Is warmed by your love.
Lord of life, help me.

In this hour
I ask to be given someone to love;
I don't want a hand to hold
But someone to love by caring.
This day must be full of people to love,
Even if only for a little time.
Help me to lift others up.
Take over my life so that when I am alone
I will not be lonely
For you will live in me.
Lord of life, come now
And help me.

MONEY WORRY

In this morning light
I seem to be obsessed
With worries about money.
I have hardly noticed
If the sky is cloudy
Or if the sun is shining.
I have eaten breakfast absent-mindedly,
I am finding it hard to concentrate
Like a man lost in a maze.
Every corner I turn
Brings me up against a dead-end
Or another bill.
Lord of the morning
I am in your presence,
I need your help;
Calm my mind.

Lord, have I got things out of proportion again?
Why do I let things get on top of me?
When I think of my family
And how much they mean to me,
When I think of the love I receive,
How stupid it is
To be depressed by a telephone bill.
When I think of your creation,
The sky is just as endless,
The sea as wide and fathomless
As it was yesterday
And will be tomorrow.
Deep down I know that the world will not end
Because of a rates demand.
Lord of the morning, help me.

Lord, help me to keep my balance,
Keep alive my sense of humour,
Help me to laugh at myself
And my ridiculous fears,
Lift me out of my maze of petty worries,
Relax my fretful mind
With its small concerns
And show me the largeness of life
That I might be grateful
In the knowledge that I am rich
In basic fundamental things.
I am alive, I love and I am loved –
What's a few bills?
Lord of the morning,
Thank you.

DISCONTENT

In this morning light
I feel the greyness of winter.
The things about me
Seem tired and worn;
There is a sameness about the pattern
Of my life
And it's hard to avoid
The tedium of my daily routine.
There are times when familiar faces
Are a comfort.
But there are times when I long
To start again,
To see new faces
To live in a different place,
To find a new way of life.

Lord, I know that there are many
Who would gladly exchange places with me,
And I feel guilty
Because I know I undervalue the work I have been
    given.
I am sometimes deliberately blind
To the richness of workaday friendship.
I know that I waste
Valuable hours of relaxation;
I let them slip through my fingers.
Lord of the morning, help me.

Lord, lift me up
With your spirit,
The spirit which gives purpose to my life,
The spirit which brings joy
Into ordinary conversation,
The spirit which brings peace of mind
In the midst of tension and fatigue,
The spirit that turns colleagues
Into friends,
The spirit that lifts familiar works and action
Into gestures and signs of love,
The spirit that renews all things,
Even me.
Lord of the morning,
Spirit of life and love, help me.

FRIENDSHIP

In this hour
I remember the face of a friend,
A friend that I haven't seen for some time
And I would like to see again.
There are so many friends I have lost touch with
And it would be so easy
To pick up a 'phone, or send a card.
Real friendship is too precious
To forget or neglect.

Lord I need friends
But I wonder what kind of a friend
I am to others.
I know I am guilty of using other people
Even people I care about deeply.
Help me to be warm in greeting people.
Help me to give, to give some love
And friendship to all the people I shall meet this day.
Lord of the morning, help me.

I am often selfish with my friends.
I want them to listen to *me*,
To *my* problems, and I only
Half listen to them.
Lord of life, forgive me.

Lord of life
Help me to be a friend,
A trustworthy friend;
To be able to defend
When others gossip or criticize.
Greater love has no man
Than when he lays down his life for his friends.
Sometimes I am not able even to lay aside
Five minutes for those who need my time.
Lord help me to realize both the gift
And the responsibility of friendship.

Lord
Help me to really look
At the people that I pass fleetingly every day,
The people on the fringe of my life.
Help me not to be enclosed
Within the inner circle of my own friends
But to offer friendship
To those who find it difficult
To make friends.
Lord of the morning, help me.

GOD BE IN MY HEAD

In this hour
Somewhere in the world
People will be meeting on buses and trains
In shops, factories and offices.
Some will meet only for a few fleeting moments,
Others will spend most of the day together.
I may meet people who will cheer me,
Make me smile or maybe annoy me.
Lord of the morning, help me.

In the hours ahead
I may bring the warmth of friendship to some,
Others I may irritate and anger.
Lord, life is too short for bitterness,
For quarrelling, or for hurtful gossip.
Yet sometimes it is hard to think kindly
About those I share my days with.
Lord of life, help me.

Through the hours of this day
I may say things that I will regret,
Things that will hurt or cause bitterness,
Yet in doing this
I hurt myself,
Spoil my own day.
Sometimes I am my own worst enemy.
In the way I think of people,
Talk to people,
Work with people,
Lord of life, help me.

Lord of life throughout this day
Take over my mind,
My words,
My actions,
My life.

God be in my head,
And in my understanding;
God be in mine eyes,
And in my looking;
God be in my mouth,
And in my speaking;
God be in my heart,
And in my thinking;
God be at mine end, and at my departing.
Amen.

ANGER

In this morning light
I'm trying to control
A feeling of anger,
Anger that is not simply in my brain
But eats its way into my very being.
I've tried to dismiss it,
And for a time I do;
Then a word, or a face
Flits across my mind
And the anger surges back.
I want to hit out
But I know that if I do
Things will be worse.
Anger is never satisfied;
It feeds on harsh words and thoughts.

I know that I should be big enough
To cope with gossiping tongues,
Innuendo, insulting words,

But I cannot ignore the fact
That they upset me, hurt me.
I don't want to be caught up
In the futility of anger,
The destructiveness of anger,
The loss of control that returns
Hurt for hurt,
The wild use of words as weapons
That break friendships
And damage lives.
Lord of the morning, help me.

Lord, I know what I should do
But doing it is another matter.
I always think of what I should have said
Afterwards
When it's too late.
It's hard to offer love in the face
Of jealousy or spite,
To resist anger,
To be a peacemaker
When popular voices are on the attack.
Lord, at least help me
Not to be the source
Of anger in others.
Throughout this day
Be with me – in my mind,
In my eyes
And on my lips.

RECONCILIATION

In this hour
There is new opportunity,
Opportunity to start again,
To forget old failures,
Old mistakes.
But where can I start
With so many mistakes to mend?
Quarrels between friends,
Thoughtless words that hurt,
Pride that makes reconciliation hard.
Lord of the morning, help me.

In this hour
Help me to make a fresh start
In my marriage,
To love through all the moments
Of joy and sadness
In good times and bad
For richer or for poorer
In sickness and in health
Till death us do part.
Help me Lord
To love and cherish
Throughout my life.
Teach me the way
Of gentleness and care.

Help me to remove the barriers
That separate
Family, friends,
Brothers, sisters,
Sons and daughters.
Teach me the way of reconciliation
That being reconciled to those about me
I might be reconciled to you.

Lord
Give me the ability
To say that I'm sorry
When I have been wrong.
Give me the words
That will heal the wounds
That I have caused in quarrelling.
Give me the wisdom to understand
Those who disagree with me.
Give me the grace
To accept another's point of view.

Lord
Fill me with your spirit
That I might, where there is hatred, give love;
Where there is injury, pardon;
Where there is doubt, faith;
Where there is despair, hope;
Where there is darkness, light;
Where there is sadness, joy.
Lord of life, help me.

TOO BUSY TO LOVE

In this morning light
I seem to be hurrying
Into the day.
I see about me
Those who share my life,
Yet in the hustle
For bathroom, breakfast and bus,
They only merit a glance
Or a brief word.
Eye on the clock
Toast in my hand
It takes too much time
To say, 'I love you.'
Lord, in the morning rush, help me.

Lord of the morning
Moments like these are rare,
Moments when I stop to ask myself,
'What am I hurrying for?'
The days are so busy,
Working, earning, getting,
That I almost have no time for living,
No time to enjoy the company
Of my wife and children.
I waste precious moments,
Moments that could live with me
For the rest of the day,
Moments when we touch or
There's a meeting of eyes.
Lord help me to be still with them
At least one moment today.

Lord in this moment of stillness
Help me to remember that I am loved
Even though I don't deserve it.
I am loved by family and friends
And amazingly, I am loved by you.

Lord of the morning
Help me to stop rushing.
I can't love my family in a hurry.
Help me to take time off
To love.

INTERCESSION

In this morning light
The streets are busy
With nameless people on their way to work.
There are faces everywhere,
Behind newspapers on trains,
Looking down from the upper windows
Of double-decker buses,
Peering through the windscreens
Of private cars.
And in each mind
There is a question that needs an answer
Or a problem that must be faced
Or a decision to be made.
Millions of people
In cities, towns and villages,
Every one is different
And yet somehow
Every one of them is me.
Lord of the morning, help us.

As this morning light
Falls in shafts
Through different windows,
It reveals a hospital ward,
Nurses, doctors, patients.
Lord, give them the strength
They need for this day.

As doors open in schools,
Factories and offices,
Men, women and children
Begin a day
That might make many demands,
Teachers in their relationships
With children,
Children with new ideas
And things to learn.
In industry, on shop floors,
In homes and at office desks
We will struggle with the business of the day.
Lord, help us.

In this morning light
My problems seem so difficult
That it is hard to find words
To express them.
Lord of the morning
Why do I seek for words
When you know the things
That are in my mind?

All I have to do
Is to say,
'Lord, look at me'.
Take the confusion out of my head,
Calm the panic
That seems to rise in my chest.
Lord, take over.
Guide me in the things
I will say and do today.
Help me in the decisions I must make.
Reassure me that your support
Is always available to me,
And that I have but to ask
And you will provide the strength
That will carry me through
Whatever this day might bring.
I am asking for your help, now.
Lord of the morning, help me.

FORGIVENESS

In this morning hour
The world listens to itself,
To the things that people like us are doing
To each other.
We shake our heads and wonder
What the world is coming to
And whether it is possible
To be forgiven for what we have done
To the world and to ourselves.
Lord of life, help us.

Forgiveness is what we need
For the grudges we hold,
For the thoughts we think,
For the words we say,
For the things we do
That hurt and disfigure
Our fellows and ourselves.
Forgiveness is what we need.

Forgiveness is what we need;
Forgiveness for man-made dust-bowls,
For earth ravaged by greed,
Forgiveness for the misuse of beauty,
For the desecration of what is rich and lovely
In exchange for what is cheap and tawdry,
For guns and bombs,
For the savage destruction
That man has wreaked for centuries;
Lord of life, help us.

You Lord are the God of mercy,
The forgiving God,
The giver of peace,
And peace of mind is what we need,
The peace that is harmony with our fellows,
Harmony with creation and the creator,
The peace that comes from mutual forgiveness –
Peace in our homes,
Peace in our hearts,
Peace in the world.

But God so loved the world
That he gave his only begotten son
That whosoever believes in him
Should not perish but have eternal life.
And we who are crippled by sin,
Deformed by selfishness,
Can, if we listen, hear the voice that says,
'Rise up: your sins are forgiven you.'

WHO – ME?

In this morning light
As I try to bring some order
Into my mind
I sometimes catch a glimpse
Of the obvious.
In a brief moment of insight
I see myself as others see me.
Not for long – I shut it out
Because I do not want to see
The unloving face that I so often show
To my wife, my children,
To the people I meet in passing
Every morning.

Lord of the morning
What blinds me
To my own shortcomings?
What incredible arrogance
Makes me see all my faults
As virtues?
I see myself as 'a bit of a perfectionist'
When others see me

As impatient and conceited.
I see myself as being modest
Or humble about my achievements
Whilst others hear me boasting.
I like to see myself doing things
For other people's good
When in fact I'm mainly concerned
About what is good for me.
I think I am a loving person
But really I am in love
With the idea of love
Not the life of love.

Love is patient and kind;
Love is not jealous or boastful;
It is not arrogant or rude.
Love does not insist on its own way;
It is not irritable or resentful;
It does not rejoice at wrong,
But rejoices in the right.
Love bears all things,
Believes all things,
Hopes all things,
Endures all things.
Love never ends.
Lord of the morning,
Help me to see love, to know love,
And to live in love.

HEARING AIDS AND WALKING STICKS

In this morning light
The young rush to school and to work
And the elderly watch them go;
Those old eyes that have loved,
That have closed tight in the agony and ecstasy
Of childbirth;
Eyes that have shared the pain and joy
Of family life;
Eyes that have looked long into the hollow pit
Of grief.

So often I talk to the elderly as if
They were children.
I give them Christmas presents of chocolates
And bars of scented soap.
I am impatient with the frailty of age,
Their slowness, their deafness, their aching bones;
Heroes with hearing aids and walking sticks,
Smelling of pipe tobacco
And lapsing into the stillness
Of minds lost in memories of the past.
These are the people who lived through wars
For me,
Suffered for me, wept for me,
Nursed me, loved me.

How dare I mutter
'Silly old thing'
Of a woman who may have given more to mankind
Than I can even imagine.
How dare I dismiss
As a 'doddering old fool'
The huffing, puffing man
Who survived torpedoed ships for me,
Lay in trenches,
Dug coal mines
For me.
Lord of the morning, forgive me.

Lord this day
Take from me
The arrogance of the modern mind.
Help me to understand,
Give me the patience to hear
The old and oft repeated stories.
Help me to learn from their experience,
To value the wisdom garnered
From the harvests of many years.
Give me the eyes to see
The beauty of age,
To learn that love and life
Are not confined to youth
But reach out to eternity.
Lord of the morning, help me.

FEELING TIRED

In this morning light
The world shakes itself awake
Like a great shaggy dog
And prepares to meet another day.
Cups and saucers rattle
And millions of homes
Are filled with the morning smell of toast.
In various places machines have started,
In factories and on farms.
People board buses and trains,
Letters are opened
And telephones start to ring.
I too should be coming alive
But somehow I feel so tired.
Lord of the morning, help me.

Lord
Why is it that so often
I start the day feeling tired?
Sometimes I know that the reason
Is simply lack of sleep,
Going to bed too late,
Staying up talking into the small hours,
And that's my fault.
But sometimes I feel tired even after
A good night's sleep.
Is it because I don't want to face work
And responsibility?
Lord of the morning
Give me the strength
To face the tasks of this day.

In this morning light
Some of the things I have to do
Seem to loom large before me,
And I carry the prospect of work
Like a heavy burden weighing me down
Even before I begin.
Yet by this evening many of today's
Difficulties will have passed.
Maybe they will prove to have been
Far less arduous than I imagined.
The thought of a problem
So often turns out to be worse
Than the problem itself.
Lord, lift my spirit,
Give me energy and a sense of humour
Throughout the hours of this day.
Lord of the morning, help me.

DAILY WORK

In this morning light
I'm thinking about my daily work.
I sometimes wonder
How I came to have my present job
Or why I earn my living
In my particular way.
Should I be doing something else with my life?
Should I be looking for something new,
Something better, or ought I to be content,
Grateful for employment
When many have no work at all?
Lord of the morning,
During this working day, guide me.

Lord, over the years I have been caught up in the
    race
For something better.
Perhaps this is the time to stop,
To stop racing ahead, to take stock.
If I have learned my trade,
If I am competent in my work
Perhaps I should stay where I am
And try to improve what I do.
Lord, is that common sense
Or simply cowardice?

Lord, throughout the hours of the day
Help me to appreciate
The work I have been given to do.
If I have talents,
Help me to use them.
Let me not waste my gifts by neglecting them
Or through craving the gifts of others.
Help me to be courageous
In decisions about the use of my time and energy
At work and at home.
Lord of the morning, help me.

BUSY DOING NOTHING

In this morning light
I feel regret
For the time that has slipped through my fingers.
Days pass so quickly.
I feel busy
Yet I seem to have done nothing.
I start a day with good intentions
But I keep putting things off.
Suddenly the day is nearly spent
And I am telling myself,
'I feel tired, I'll do it tomorrow'.
Sometimes I suspect
I am putting off living.
Lord of the morning, help me.

Lord sometimes
I am like a man walking up
And down saying,
'I'm busy, I'm very busy,
I've got so many things to do.
I haven't got time for the thing that I'm doing now'.

But how long does it take
To live now?
How long does it take
To notice somebody?
How long does it take
To send a card to say,
'Thinking of you'?
How long does it take
To look at a flower,
To smile, and say a prayer?
Lord of the morning, help me.

Lord, help me to work out
The things I have to do today.
There are probably only
One or two really important things.
Give me the courage
To tackle those things first
And then show me
That I do have time
To listen,
Time for kindness,
Time for laughter,
Time for love.
Lord of the morning,
Help me not to be
Too busy to live.

TOMORROW AND ITS NEEDS

In this morning light
Lies the day ahead.
All my apprehensions and fears,
My hopes and longings
Rise up once more.
Sometimes I am almost overwhelmed
At the thought of starting again.
Little things bother me:
What clothes to wear,
What bus or train to catch.
How will I manage today,
With the bigger things,
With people and events?
Lord of the morning, help me.

In this morning light
Are the faces of those I will meet
At the newsagents,
In travel,
At work,
Over coffee and lunch.

And I am anxious – for success,
To please, to be loved – self-centred.
It's hard to turn about,
To let others please me,
To love others because *they*
Need loving,
Not because of what's in it for me.
Lord of the day, help me.

In this morning light
I look ahead
As always,
Always to the future,
Never now.
Always the next problem
Instead of this moment of peace.
It's hard to enjoy *now*, *today*,
Because it's not just the next problem
But tomorrow's problems
Which sometimes never happen.

Lord, help me not to let my life
Revolve about the possible trials of tomorrow.
Give me the courage to resist the temptations
That will stand before me today
So that today may have moments
When I may be counted worthy
Of the Lord of my hours, my minutes,
My life.
Lord of the morning, help me.

MY WORLD

In this morning light
My sleep-laden eyes are reluctant
To meet the hurly-burly of the world.
Lord, help me to get my world into perspective.
What is my world?
My home? My family? My friends?
All of them I suppose.
The people who support me every day
By their presence,
Who share my problems,
Argue with me, eat with me,
Criticize me, laugh with me,
Love me – these are my family,
My world.

Lord, I know that I have a responsibility
To a bigger world;
But help me not to forget how much
I need those who share the ordinary things of every
    day.
And do not let me pass by those who are lonely,
Because of shyness, or age, or some handicap.
Lord, help me to be grateful
For the people I call 'family'
And help me to be open
To anyone who wants to share some time
With me today.

Lord of the morning
My small world
Is only a fraction of a bigger world.
Help me to remember
The responsibilities that I have to brothers and sisters
From different races, creeds and countries;
Brothers and sisters that I have never met
But who are affected by how I live,
By the money I earn, or spend, or give,
Who suffer because of my apathy.
And let me not forget, that they are my brothers and
    sisters
Because you are the Father of the family of man.
Lord of the morning, help me.

BEING ALIVE

In this morning light
I am trying to see
What day it is.
Sometimes I seem to lose a day,
And it's a bit frightening
When I can't remember where the day went to
Or what happened to the week.
And birthdays come so fast
That I have to work out how old I am.
Lord of the morning,
I don't want my life to trickle away
Like water on sand.
I don't want to waste this day;
I want to live it. Help me.

Lord of the morning
The days that are lost
Are usually the days
When I have forgotten to stop and speak to you
In prayer,
When the hours and minutes
Have been so busy
That you have been crowded out of my life.

These are the lost days.
It's strange
But I only live my life
When I'm prepared to give it away.
The only days I keep
Are the days I am willing
To give to you.
It's a curious paradox.
I want to live
Yet I have to let *me* die
Before I can start living.
Lord of the morning, help me.

In this morning light
There is peace.
It is the peace of your presence.
In this morning light
There is sensitivity
Because of your Spirit.
In this morning light
There is power, strength, life.
It is the life that you give.

Lord, help me to give this day to you
So that I might really live.
Help me to say when things are difficult,
'Lord, this day is your day
And I belong to you.'
Lord of the morning,
Help me to live.

I WISH I HADN'T DONE THAT

In this morning light
My conscience is nagging me.
There is something I have to put right, today.
Yesterday I lost my temper
With someone I love.
It wasn't simply anger,
I lost my temper, lost control,
Allowed frustration and weariness
To burst out in a flood
Of stupid, venomous words;
And this morning the bitterness
Of the hurt I inflicted is still with me.
Lord of the morning, help me.

Lord, I know that I can make excuses,
Add up all the pressures of the day,
Of the week, and say
It was just the last straw,
I couldn't help it.
But that wouldn't be true,
I wouldn't have indulged
In that uncontrollable rage
With my employer, or people I wanted to impress.
No, I had to do it to someone
Who loves me
Because deep down inside
I knew that I would still be loved
Even as you love me,
In spite of my weaknesses.

Lord of the morning
I know that one of the privileges
Of being loved
Is to be able to let off steam
In the presence of those I love.
I know that the release
Of pent up feelings
Can be a cleansing process,
But help me not to exploit love;
Help me in recognizing the love
That embraces me
To be changed by that love
To give love in return
This day.
Lord of the morning, help me.

A DAY TO REMEMBER

In this morning light
The faces of my family
Smile at me from a photograph
And I find myself smiling back.
A fleeting moment of happiness
Trapped on a film
Bringing me happiness now.
At this moment I can hear them
Moving about the house,
Preparing for another day.
Today there will be difficulties and problems,
Maybe we will argue, as people do.
But today Lord
Let there be moments of happiness.

In this morning light
I remember an act of kindness,
A gesture of love from a small child.
I remember laughing
Until the tears ran down our faces;
I remember the excitement,
The shouting, the rocking of the boat
When we landed our first fish.
I remember Christmas trees
And birthday parties,
Sunny days on the beach,
Wet days tramping over hills.
Lord of the morning,
Help me to remember these moments
With gratitude as I go about
The ordinary things of today.

Lord of the morning
If happiness is sharing,
Loving, giving, understanding,
Help me to share the good things of this day.
Help me to be loving
And thoughtful with family and friends.
Help me to be generous in giving
Time and attention.
Help me to be understanding
When things go wrong
So that this day will be a day of love,
A day to remember.
Lord of the morning, help me.

CHILDREN

In this hour
All over the world
Mothers and fathers
Are thinking about
Their children
And worrying about them.
How are they getting on at school,
With their friends, with their work;
And after school
In their leisure?
What will they do?
How will they mature?
What sort of people will they become?
What will they do with their lives?
You have given us the gift of children,
Lord, guide us, to say and do the right
Things for them,
To be near them when they want us,
To love them, no matter what they may do.
Lord of the morning, help us.

In this hour
School teachers prepare lessons for our children,
Work out schedules
Plan particular lessons
For particular children

Good children, sad children, happy children,
Awkward children, funny children –
Our children.
Together, parent and teacher
We will influence them
These children,
How they think, speak and act.
These are the days
In which we will lay the foundations
Of their lives,
Surrounding them with the things that matter:

Love, laughter and joy,
Even bitterness, anger and sorrow.
Lord of life, help us.

Lord
Help us to be patient
With our children,
To give them time
When they need it,
To listen to their views
However much they may differ from ours.
Help us in our conversations together
That we may always trust each other.
As our children search for knowledge
Help us to learn with them.

Lord of life
As we try to help and guide our children,
We realize how much
We need help and guidance ourselves.
We call upon you, as our Father,
And ask for the help of your spirit.
It was said,
'If you know how to give
Good gifts to your children,
How much more will the heavenly Father
Give the Holy Spirit
To those who ask him'.
Lord, fill us with your spirit
For our sake
And for the sake of our children.

NEW YEAR

In this morning light
The old year is dying;
Even now the troubles of last year
Are fading into the past to be forgotten,
Yet there is so much to be remembered with
    gratitude.
In this coming year
I'd like to be able to sort out my life,
To throw away yesterday's mistakes
And keep the good things.
Yet I need yesterday's mistakes.

A new year is coming
And fresh hope;
I was never any good at making resolutions,
Perhaps I made too many.

I can't count the things I was *going* to do,
Or stop doing, or give up.
But I'm reluctant to give up anything.
I cling to the things I want,
Forgetting that fragile gifts
Held in a possessive grip usually break.
Lord, help me not to cling so fiercely
To the things I claim as mine
When even the breath I breathe is yours.
Lord of the morning,
Help me to give back the life I owe to you.

In this morning light
Give me courage to offer this year
And everything in it to you.
The things I may enjoy
Or the things I may suffer,
The hours in which I may be used
Or *not* used by you.
Let me from this day
Put my whole life into your hands –
Triumphs and failures,
Laughter and tears,
They are all at your disposal.
From this minute
Let me be no longer my own,
But yours.
Lord of the morning, help me.

THE VOYAGE OF THE MILLER

This poem was written one winter while sailing on the North Sea in a schooner called the Malcolm Miller.

When evening had come, he said to them, 'Let us go across to the other side'. And leaving the crowd, they took him with them just as he was, in the boat. And other boats were with him. And a great storm of wind arose, and the waves beat into the boat, so that the boat was already filling. But he was in the stern, asleep on the cushion. *(Mark 4: 35–38 RSV.)*

Was it ever quiet?
Were we ever still?
Were all our days a
Continuous struggle
For mastery of the storm?

Gusts of passion drove us from youth,
Love was tempestuous
And the gentle softness of our years
Wounded deeply;
Scars healed and hardened us,
Taught us, and turned us
Into shellbacks
Surviving in a sea of fears.

Was it ever quiet?
Were we ever still
As we made our passage
From ignorance to knowledge,
Still for long enough
To see the stars before us,
To feel the tide,
To plot a course,
However rough and ready:
Or did we hurl ourselves
Against the breakers,
Blind within the foam,
Clasping hands with those about us,
Struggling for a foothold
On slipping, shifting, shingle stone?

A bitter brine washed us then,
A wet and cold reality
That cooled the ecstasy
Of experience.
And here,
Aloft in the arms

Of the Miller's rigging,
Over a grey green sea,
I search the horizon
For the elusive stillness
That I long for, yearn for,
Hope for,
A moment of seeing quietness
In my head.

But it's never quiet here,
In the mind,
Not in this vast storehouse
Of all our days,
Of images, voices, laughter,
Of pain's intensity;
Not with an army of experiences
Tramping through the brain.
Even in our therapeutic sleep
Doors open and shut.
In the labyrinth of memory
There are signposts,
Symbols of the event.
A hand, a smile, a face,
A tree with snow-laden leaves
And we slip and slide
On a cerebral trip
To childhood.

Not what you would call quiet,
This crowded playground
Of shouting ideas,

Jumping, running thoughts,
And questions
Playing hopscotch
On the cobbles of conscience.
All our days
From that first, blind kicking
Exit from the womb,
And earlier,
When ear was pressed to belly
To feel and hear
The jerk of embryonic life,
And before that,
When did the moulding start?
When did we hear
The voice of our mothers?
Where did we begin?
Who am I?

How brief
The furious storms
That tossed that adolescent sea;
How short-lived
The righteous anger
That drifts astern
In the wake of age.
There was no quietness there,
No stillness worth remembering,
Just fitful prayers
That filled the occasional lull.

The zealous vows of puberty
Scarce die on the wind
When away on the port beam
Another zephyr is sighted,
A shadowy ripple on the surface of the sea,
Moving swiftly, inexorably, towards us;
Followed by a grey black
Impenetrable mass
That will soon engulf the ship,
And then – she strikes!
We fight to shorten sail,
Heeled hard over
Bows slice through waves
And crash into rollers,
Churning up a wide spreading patch
Of frothing water.
We clutch at shroud and stay,
Bend our heads
Against the shrieking, fearful wind
And in spite of all,
It is grand, grand,
This struggle for survival,
Grand to realize,
To learn, to know the strength
Of muscle and sinew,
Thought and deed.

This is what we came for,
To live to the brim,
To fight the battle,
To plunge into careers,
Marriage, children, property,
Laughter, tears, pain and death.

Here is the great storm,
Life itself.
Sails tear, timbers split,
Head and hands and feet
Are wounded,
Yet still we try to stem the storm.
The ship is filling
And we must bail and pump
Till our backs ache,
For this ship is the only one we have,
This voyage is the only one we make,
And this power that drives us
Is the majesty that drives the sea.

The sea is full of people
People who struggle and weep,
People who triumph and laugh,
People who suffer and despair.
For some the days and nights are harsh
Filled with frightful cacophony;
For some there is music
That brings sense
To the madness of the maelstrom.

But who tunes the ears
That hear the sounds
That spirits make?
What notes pierce the traffic roar,
The din of markets, money and men?
Why this carpenter,
This fisherman, this dentist,
This lawyer, farmer, teacher, priest?
Why him, why her, why me
To hear the irresistible sound
Of that small voice?
How comes the deafness
Of those who do not hear?
Are lives more wicked
Or time more wasted?
Which office-worker is measurably
More good than his fellow?
Which steeplejack is nearer to God?
Which baker moulds pastry
With a holier hand?
Do they choose
Or are they chosen
To hear the whisper
That never dies?

And the waves beat into the boat
So that the boat was already filling,
But he was in the stern, asleep
On the cushion.

And now it is evening
And the day is far spent,
Tired and weary
We are ready to admit defeat.
We are broken, beaten
And fearful of death.
Yet can it be
That he who drives the sea
Sails with us?
Has he shared
The storm and all its alarms
And now sleeps in the stern
Without worry, without fear?
Who is he who sleeps in the
Face of fury?
Can this be the one who has power
Over the storm?
Can this be the one who can
Still the waves,
Who has power over life itself?
We have tried to sail
Against the wind
On each and every day
In our own strength,
In youth and maturity,
Yet throughout those years
Has he been with us?
With us in the storm,
Waiting for us to turn to him,
Waiting to be asked
To still the waves.

Lord
Forgive me for living my life
As if you were not present.
For trusting in my own strength
And not yours.
Teach me to trust you
Especially when the journey
Seems difficult and hard.
Give me peace
That cannot be disturbed
By the fiercest storm.
Give me the knowledge
That no matter how many problems
May strew the way ahead
You who have the power
To still the storm
Can bring strength and stillness
Into my life.

LORD
of my
days

PRAYING

Lord of my days
I have so often said, 'Teach me to pray.'
As a child I learned the prayer of prayers,
The Lord's Prayer.
I committed to memory
The great traditional prayers of the church.
They have been a foundation
And support for all my prayers.
But there are times when words fail me,
When all the prayers I've ever heard or read
Seem inappropriate,
And the jumble of thoughts,
Worries, questions,
Rushing through my head
Reduce me to silence,
Or the single plea,
'Lord, help me.'

Time has taught me
That I can pray without words.
You, who number the hairs on my head,
Know my every thought.

You know the decisions I must make,
Every problem, every failure,
Every triumph, every joy
Is known to you.
And it is enough to close my eyes,
To come into your presence and say,
'Lord, you know what is happening to me,
In my work, in my marriage,
In my mind and in my body.
Loving Lord, help me.'

Sometimes I have felt guilty
That I have not expressed my gratitude
For the love I have received.
But now I know
That I do not need to find acceptable words.
I need only be aware of you.
I see now that when music moves me to tears
It is because I have perceived your presence in the
    melody.
When, in a moment of drama,
Or at the peak of an artist's performance,
I feel a shiver running down my spine,
It is because your Spirit is passing through me.

A peal of warm-hearted laughter
Is a response to your love
Living in people,
And now at last I dimly see
That prayer is not only words
But a way of living,

An awareness of your presence,
A perception of the power of your Spirit in my life;
Supporting me,
Healing me,
Loving me.
Lord
Teach me to pray
With my life.

THE COMPANY OF HEAVEN

How many years had I looked
At sandstone rocks, red and soft,
Scoured by wind,
Engraved with lovers' initials and dates,
And never noticed that the earth beneath the grass
Was the same rich red.

I saw its redness that day,
Felt its coarse dryness in my hands
As we stood around and prayed.
Prayed with the wind on our faces
For the passing of my father.
The voice of the priest
Mingled with the breeze and birdsong
But in my head was the music of memory,
Voices, songs, stories
Sounding again and again in my mind,
And I knew
That he was not there,
Not beneath the flowers,
Not beneath the gaze of our bowed heads,
And yet he was with us
As he had never been before.
He, his brothers and sisters
And all the company of heaven
Reassuring us of a promise fulfilled.

In my Father's house are many mansions
And I go to prepare a place for you
So that where I am, you may be also;
If it were not so I would have told you.
And suddenly, in my mind's eye, I saw them,
Two tromboning brothers
Laughing whilst counting the rest bars
In the music of eternity.

The refrain was familiar
Yet I could not catch the tune,
And knew I never would
Not as long as I stood here
Or walked the journey of my days.
But the words, I knew,
At least the prelude to that unfinished masterpiece
Whose opening chorus begins,
The eye has not seen
Nor the ear heard,
Nor has it entered the heart of man
What things have been prepared
For those who love God.

And there
With that red earth beneath my feet,
I knew
That nothing could separate me
From the love of Christ
Or the love of those
Whose song, even now,
Is singing in my soul.

THE THINGS THAT LAST

People were living here
Before the Romans came marching past the
    grocers,
The library and the bank.
The horse and ass and oxen
Pulled their weight through the gate in the wall
Where the buses change their crew.

Beneath the tarmacadam at your feet
You can feel the cobblestones
That broke the wooden wheel and the shoes
Of priest and tinker on their rounds.

The tallest and the oldest building still in use
Is the flying buttressed church
That suffered such abuse
From Cromwell's iconoclastic troops.

And all around are towers, tiles and chimneys
That felt the rain
That fell upon the faces of our parents
Before our days began.
Steps and stones,
Worn down brass plates
Declaring partners in law long at rest.

Windows and doors
Locking out and shutting in
The din of voices past and present.
Traders trade from market stall
To superstore with multi-level car parks.
In the street a meter-maid stands
Where silk-gloved hands assisted ladies
From their carriages.

Then as now
Men and women worried, argued and prayed
To a God outside of time
To whom a thousand years
Is but the twinkling of an eye.
Each of us in our short space
Will leave a mark.
The things we build,
From semi-detached to high rise flat,

May say something of our industry.
But the things that last
Cannot be measured in bricks and mortar.
For how old is sacrifice?
What age is faith?
How long does courage live?
When does hope end?

Lord
May the warmth and laughter and hope
That I have known
Be handed down in trust
To my children, and children to come.
May they live to know
That whilst all things fade and die,
Love lives on.

A ROSE IN A BOTTLE

Behold the lilies of the field;
Solomon in all his glory
Was not arrayed as one of these.

And behold a rose
Not in a garden
Or in some florist's artfully bound bouquet,
But in a bottle
A milk bottle in a kitchen
With the sounds of the dishes,
The radio and the children at breakfast.
A rose in a bottle
Startling among the cereals and marmalade,
As if in the midst of our domestic reality
A greater reality had sprung up
Between the salt and pepper and the butter dish.

Through the window is the garden,
Leaves and grass and roses.
Outside the window,
Beyond the cat washing his ears,
Is the garden I have seen so often
And yet so often do not see.
But this single flower
This rose in a bottle
Demands my attention.

Each velvet smooth petal
Softly curved and rounded,
Each subtle change of colour
From leaf and stem
To the depth of its bloom
Draws me closer
Until I am bewitched by the fragrance
That belongs only to this particular flower.
And there it stands between teapot and toast
Telling me that today
I shall not see anything more beautiful.

Lord
Let me not be blind
To the beauty I will see today.
Let me see the beauty
That I usually ignore
In people.
In between the queues for buses and trains,
In between the telephone calls
And the voices of friends and colleagues
Let me see beauty,
In words spoken with thought and care
In a job well done
In a single gesture of kindness.

Today you have shown me the beauty of a rose
In a bottle,
In an ordinary kitchen.
Let me see also the flower of love
That you have planted in ordinary people.

FIELDS

It's just a field
An English field in summer.
Beneath my head is grass,
Green and cloverleaf.
In my eyes and on my face
Dappled shadows,
Sunlight filtered through leaves of silver birch
Shimmering on a gentle breeze.
In my ears, the sounds of insects,
Grasshoppers, crickets,
Dragonflies and bees
Humming and hovering in heat and haze,
Exploring the hearts of flowers
Wild and sturdy in the hedgerows.
And in my head
The scent of fresh cut grass
Soothing the intrusive thoughts
Of a mind that never rests.

And it's just a field
An English field in summer.

A county, surrounded by mist grey hills,
Stretches like a patchwork quilt
Of greens and browns and golds
Stitched by hedges and lanes,
Decorated with cattle and sheep,
Knotted together with whitewalled cottages,
Farmyards and barns.

Deep, rural, harvest seedbeds
Pushing up from rain-rich soil,
Grain, corn, barley, oats and hay,
Filling the shelves of supermarkets,
The pantries of suburban semis.

Bread on the breakfast table.

Yet not by bread alone shall we live
Here in this field
Like the wind playing with the grass
Blows the Spirit.
The Spirit that brought forth the world
From the void of space,
The breath of life that feeds me
So that I shall never hunger.
In this very breath that I breathe
Is the mystery of all created things,
In this field
This English field in summer.

SKY

Lord of life
There is no part of your creation
That does not speak of the wonder of your being.
Day by day
We walk and laugh and live
Beneath the changing endless sky.
In cities, in countryside,
Or beyond the land
Where sea and sky marry
In mysterious union of height and depth,
Reflecting moon and stars and rising sun
When those with ears can hear
The sons of morning singing for joy.
And yet, how often have I missed
The songs of heaven,
With eye and mind tuned only
To morning news
And the fleeting hands of clocks.

Beneath the dome of heaven
The sky continues her dance
With shapes and changing colour.

From first light to dawn
The world is created once again from darkness.
Out of mists and shadows
The sun in splendour beyond the reach of kings
Breathes life into the world.
His feathered cirro-stratus train trails
Aloof to robust cumulus running before the bustle
Of the south-west wind.
And in the night
Stars stand sentinel until dawn.
Moonlight caresses hills, ships
And dreaming lovers
In the endless, everchanging drama
Played above the heads of people
Boarding trains, washing cars,
Buying, selling, sleeping unaware
Of imprisonment
Or the snare of smaller things.

Lord of all created things
Let me lift up my eyes just once this day.
May the passing problems of my waking hours
Be reduced to their proper size and place
Beneath the infinite sky.
May I know your presence,
Feel and breathe the breath of life
Which is your daily gift,
And may I see
In the beauty of the heavens
The measure of your love.

THE RIVER

High on a hill and looking down
I can see a river,
Wide and meandering,
Straddled by bridges,
Alive with all kinds of craft.

Sailing boats, motor-boats,
Pilot boats, police launches,
Harbour Authority vessels
Manoeuvering with all the grace
Of water-borne things,
Barges, lighters, coasters,
And cargoes of timber down from the north.

Flags that have fluttered
In Spanish harbours and Baltic ports
Fly over men speaking different tongues.
And the river bears them all
Swirling beneath their bows
Beer cans, plastic bottles
And all the flotsam of industry.

High on this hill
I can see the fields and green banks
That embraced the river in her youth,
And somewhere,
Beyond the rolling green horizon
The water rises in crystal innocence,
Sparkling over stones,
Dreaming beneath the willow
And listening to the thrill of meadow-pipit,
Lark and thrush.

Below me is my river, reflecting all my days
From the running, fresh quickness of childhood
To the slower, broader surge of strength,
Held in check by the ebb and flow of experience,
And beyond the estuary is the sea
And eternity.

Lord of life
Carry me through the river of my days.
Let me not be wearied
By an endless tide of demands
Or overwhelmed by the swirling pressures
Of the mainstream of my years,

But let me glimpse the enormity of your purpose
For every living soul,
And for me.
Let me live in the hope of your promise
That lies beyond the far horizon.

NOT A SPARROW FALLS

We heard them first
A whirring, rhythmic throb,
A steady beat of majestic wings
And suddenly
A squadron of swans,
Long necks extended,
Flew low over their reedy river.
We held our breath, pulses racing
In an excitement of joy and fear,
For they were both graceful
And menacing in their power.

Beneath them, unmoved,
A family of mallard ducks
Paddle between the reeds in the slow green water.
The shadow and sound of the swans fade.
Now we can hear the squeak and scurry
Of moorhens and coots
And see the surprised, indignant head
Of a crested grebe.
Swifts and swallows dive and dart
Feeding on the wing.
In the tree and out of sight
A robin sings a song
That is bigger than the bird,
Sweet and rich in pitch and variation.

Distantly
There is a continuous sound,
A rumble or buzz,
And it is hard to realise
That a mile or two away
Cars and vans and lorries
Are rushing into towns and cities;
That people are queueing and jostling,
Conveyor belts are endessly moving,
Whilst telephones ring
In shops, offices and homes.
We seem to be in separate worlds,
Unaware of each other.

Yet not a sparrow falls
Without my heavenly Father knows it.

Swans and geese and winding rivers,
Streets and lights and rivers of humanity
All fall beneath his gaze.
To him there is no secret world.

Not a sigh falls
Without he hears it.
Not a duck dives
Without he sees it;
Aches and pains are felt,
Birdsong is heard.
The miracle of the creator's love
Lies in his constant, caring presence.
No one ever weeps alone,
Worries alone,
Suffers alone,
Dies alone.
He who is aware of the meanest of his creatures
Has promised,
Fear not,
The hairs on your head are numbered,
And you are of more value than many sparrows.

REVERENCE FOR LIFE

In the first hour of light
When milk vans tour deserted streets
Purring like electric cats,
Breaking the silence with a clank of crates
Or the rattle of bottles,
Before alarm clocks shatter our dreams,
The creatures that live by meadow,
Hedge and riverbank
Have begun their struggle
To survive another day.

Otters begin their river patrol,
Deer, sensitive and alert,
Step their delicate way to secret pools.
Moles, voles, hares and rabbits
Sniff the air for warning signs of danger
Before scurrying to forage for food and drink.
Skylarks sing and eagles soar,
Black-backed gulls glide over sea and cliff,
Dippers dip and waders wade in fen and marsh.

Herons begin their morning walk
For all the world like elderly clerics
Hands clasped behind their backs
Deep in godly conversation.

And everything that moves and breathes
And flies, or walks or swims,
Is ours, our responsibility.
What is man that thou art mindful of him?
Yet thou hast given him dominion
Over the birds of the air
And the beasts of the field,
Yea, over every living thing.
But is a battery hen a living thing
Or merely a machine for making money?
Is a whale the greatest mammal of the oceans
Or simply a source of oil and fats?
Lord, forgive us for the blindness
That rips out hedgerows
Poisons the air
Pollutes our rivers
Plasters beach and bird
In the name of progress or profit.

You have made us stewards,
Entrusted us with the wonders of your creation.
Help us.
Instil within our minds
A reverence for every living thing
Lest in the hardness of our hearts
We lose our reverence for life itself.

ON THURSTASTON HILL

When we were boys we cycled to Thurstaston
Where the common was wild with shrubs
And purple flower and red sand rock.
Knights, come to the jousting field,
Our armour, flannel and tweed
With leather patched elbows;
Our helmets, peaked caps
Emblazoned with a grammar school badge.

Chase and skirmish filled the long afternoon
'Til weary of battle
We made the ascent
To the top of Thurstaston Hill
To stand like breathless conquerors
And stare across the estuary of the Dee
To the blue mists of Wales and its northern
    mountains.

Up on this hill
Where clean wind flipped our ties over our
    shoulders,
We were free,
Free from the trammels of theorems and French
    verbs,
Free from the tyranny of detentions
And six of the best.

Somehow, the wind on the hill
Filled us with an exultation
That could not be contained,
And we released it
By throwing back our heads and laughing.
Since then
The hills have shown me, again and again,
The proper size of the world below.

Not for nothing
Are there monasteries in mountains,
Nor was it by chance
That Christ climbed the hills
To struggle with his spirit
And bring order to his mind.
God forgive me
When I cannot lift my thoughts
Above the lowness of petty debate.
Forgive me
When I allow my mind
To linger in the marshlands
Of anger or suspicion.

Forgive me
That I cannot rise above attempts
To score off my friends,
When I fail to resist a base desire
To return blow for blow over some trivial matter.
Forgive me
When I allow myself to be depressed
By wallowing in the misfortune of a passing day.

I learned the lesson as a child
On Thurstaston Hill,
And it is not less true now.
In my heart I know
That when I lift up my eyes to the hills
I feel in my face a wind,
Fresh with love, alive with hope.
A wind that blows through worries
And leaves behind such a sense of the ridiculous
That once again, I am a child on a hill
Laughing in your presence.

ON A BEACH

On summer's day on every beach
From Blackpool to Bognor,
From Brighton to Bridlington,
The British paddle in the sea,
Make sandcastles and lie in deckchair ease
To the sound of breakers, seagulls
And shouting, squealing infants
Catching crabs in rocky pools,
Or digging channels
In vain attempts to stem the sea.

So many faces, yet so familiar.
Eyes hazel or blue;
Hair, blonde, brown or black;
Skin, fresh, freckled, pink,

Or darkest brown,
All reminding me of friends and family.
She could be my grandmother,
In profile that could be my Uncle George,
That voice sounds like my sister,
That walk belongs to cousin Jack.
All of us are related
Not in looks alone but in our lives,
Our fears and anxieties, our hopes and dreams,
Our passions, our pains, our pleasures.
Oh, some have better beach chairs
Or more expensive clothes,
And some have bigger mortgages,
Their faces tell you that.
Some have found the going hard,
You can see it in their eyes;
Yet, on a summer's day
We share the air, the sand and sea.
Individuals, yet united
In our frail humanity.

Why do I think I am special?
How did I come to think
That the world revolved around me?
I am never alone in any experience.
If I feel pain, so do millions more.
If I am anxious about my children,
Or money, or work,
Why do I hug it to myself
And think that life has singled out me
For special treatment?

Lord, help me to use my trials,
My needs, my failures, my successes,
My gifts, perhaps especially my suffering,
Not to measure myself
But to understand, to love,
To be able to share in the same struggles
That those around me are living through.
For the people on this beach
Are not distantly related to me –
We are all brothers and sisters,
Brown, black, blonde and pink.
Our only purpose
Is to learn to live in love
As children of God.

THE SILENT WITNESSES

Every year I see a miracle.
A dry, dead-looking bunch of twigs
Knarled and old throughout the winter,
An ancient, derelict bush,
Slowly
Comes to life again.

In April or May there are tiny buds
Whose tips show faintly green
On the withered branches.
As May advances on June
Fresh, clean, green leaves reach for the light.
In July I can no longer see
The horny old sticks of its skeleton
For they are covered with leafy finery.
In August, huge, pale purple blooms
Lift their heads to the sun
In final triumph over the dead days of winter.

My bush, my back-garden miracle
Is only one of thousands of millions
Of resurrections,

Throughout the country
In towns and cities,
In streets, parks and fields
There are thousands and thousands
Of silent witnesses to the mystery of creation.
Every bush, tree, blossom, fruit, nut and berry
Soundlessly shouts, 'See, I live!'

All around us is a great army
So quiet, so numerous, so common,
That we do not see them.
Apple, plum, pear and cherry;
Hazel nuts on wild hazel hedges,
Conkers high on horse-chestnut branches,
Sweet chestnuts to roast in winter,
How is it that we do not hear
Every leaf and branch singing songs of praise?
Exotic tulip trees, stately ash
And aspen, the quivering tree;
Copper beech, silver birch and fir;
Oak, the monarch of the forest
Who from humble acorns gave the timber
That floated Nelson's navy.
Churchyard yews, reaching back
In supple strength
To the long-bows of Agincourt.
Tree after tree has watched battles being fought,
Sheltered fugitives and lovers,
Seen the pain and joy of generations
And covered their years with autumn after
    autumn.

Lord, in my short and hurried day
May I pause for long enough to touch a leaf,
Or breathe the fragrance of a flower.
And in that moment
May I be in quiet communion
With your endless, life-giving love.

THE WEEDS OF TIME

In cracks and grooves,
Beside the thundering wheels of trains,
Grass and weed and wild flowers
Reach down into untended earth.
Hardy and tough they defy
The grey of steel and concrete
With gentle greens and blues and yellows.

Derelict houses, ruins of abbey and castle
Are softly clothed by creeper and clover,
Nettle and old man's beard,
Until, in time, only a grassy mound
Remains to remind us of the passing power of
    man.

Golden fields rich with harvest
Have heard the roar of cannon
And the cries of mortal combat.
Gentle pools and lakes
Cover places where, in sweated labour,
Men have gouged the earth
For clay and chalk and lime.
Warriors and conquerors
Built fortresses and towers
In their brief glory;
Yet the sun has set on all their labours
And grass and weed and tree and shrub
Have reasserted their claim to hold the land.

Lord
My day is very brief
And my sight is short.
A thousand years in your sight
Is like the twinkling of an eye,
For you are the infinite creator.
You dwell in eternity,
You are the beginning and the end.
Yet you have made me in your image.
You call me to enjoy eternity with you.

To you there is no past, or future,
All is one.
The saints who have gone before
And those who are yet to come
Are all part of your kingdom
Where everything that is good
And true and lovely
Is gathered into eternity.

Lord
Each day I live
Is another opportunity
To do something beautiful
For your eternal world.
Help me to see
That an act of love or kindness,
However small or simple,
Will never rust or decay
Or be covered by the weeds of time.

AN AUTUMN PRAYER

In such a place I could not speak
For leaf and lichen declared this holy ground,
A sanctuary.
Sweet chestnuts were falling,
Green, prickly spheres
Bursting apart on leaf-layered earth.
Acorns, pale and immature,
Spattered the ground around the oak.
My shoes depressed
The rain-soaked moss and glistening grass,
Footsteps hushed in the stillness of the trees.
Until, passing through
I came into the open
And like a rich symphonic chord falling on the
    ears,
My eyes were assailed with colours that sang
Chromatic scales of gold, and yellow and amber.
Leaves of brown and red and green
Raised praise to their creator
For the gift of deep and mellow autumn.

And it was lavish,
As the love of God always is.
This nature is his nature,
Extravagantly generous.
Like autumn leaves his blessings fall
And all creation
Acknowledges the love that never dies.
Only the blind of heart and mind
Cannot or will not,
See the love that wept
And hung upon a tree.

Lord
Let me reflect the colours of your love.
Let my life be bright with laughter,
My speech be gentle,
My thinking warm,
My actions kind.
May all I suffer or enjoy,
In the spectrum of my days,
Mellow and blend
In peace
In love
In praise.

A LIGHT IN THE DARK

The breeze died to a whisper,
Sails flapped, listless,
And the wind was gone.
Not a ripple remained
On the surface of the sea.
The little ship drifted
On a smooth, gently rolling surface
With her mast mirrored in the water,
An undulating reflection.
All around was silken serenity
Like an inland lake.
Yet the shores of this vast pool
Lay beyond our vision.

Even from the crosstrees of the mast
Nothing would be seen.
We took in the sails
And before the drift of the sea
Took us far off course
Started the engine
And put-put-puttered towards the horizon.

As darkness came we stared ahead
Hoping to sight a conical buoy,
A mariner's signpost.
But with darkness came the wind.
Hoisting sail we shut down the engine
And heard again the chuckle of the sea
Against the hull,
Saw the phosphorescent gleam
Of water broken by our bow.
Until then we had felt alone
But now, far off,
We could see the winking lights
Of fellow travellers,
Green and red and masthead white.
The wind backed and raced down on us.
Holding the squall in her sails
The ship leaned on her shoulder
And plunged into the waves
Throwing foam white water over the foredeck
And we pitched into the night.
For hour after hour we struggled
With sails and wind and sea.
Somehow we missed the flashing light

That would have fixed our place
In this wild night.
We feared that we were lost,
Had made an error in our reckoning,
And behind a façade of firm-faced confidence,
We prayed, and worked,
Until we saw the light.
Not the one we were expecting,
But another, greater light
That marked the land, havens and rest.

And there always is a light
As we plot our way through weeks and years,
Through the storms of our calling,
Through failure and disappointment,
Even in the dark nights of suffering,
Even in the face of death,
We pray, and there is light,
A greater light than we expected,
Guiding us to havens and to rest.

THE RHYTHM OF
NATURAL THINGS

There was a time
When man fell on his knees
And worshipped the sun.
There was a time
When the awesome grandeur
Of towering mountains
Made men pay homage
To a God of hills and peaks,

And those who ventured on the sea
Saw the terrifying power
Of the God of the vast and endless deep.
The earth itself could play with men,
Could graciously deign
To flower with fruit and corn,
Milk and honey,
Or turn towards them a barren face
Hardened with the merciless gaze
Of drought and famine.
So men made sacrificial tribute to mother earth
And prayed to her for a favourable harvest.

Primitive, unsophisticated man,
Yet was he nearer the truth than he knew?
I speak of him
As if I had never been moved by mountains,
Never felt that primeval stirring, deep inside,
At the sight of a majestic sky.
Never shivered at night, far from land,
On a moody, darkly surging sea.
Never felt the prickly fear of things invisible.

The Word was made flesh and dwelt amongst us,
And the Word was with God and the Word was
     God.

In a particular year, the Word took flesh.
Yet that Word existed, and exists
Outside of time, before time;
And moon and stars and earth and sea

From which we may have emerged,
The whole of creation
Is an expression of the nature of God.
And the simple seed that dies
And lies in autumn soil
To rise to life in spring
Is an echo of the Word of God.

Lord
Let me not be so removed
From the rhythm of natural things
That I fail to hear you
Speaking to me in the wind;
So cushioned by mechanical comforts
That I fail to feel your power
In the warmth of the sun.
So bedazzled by the brilliance
Of man's invention
That I fail to see your light in a morning sky.
Lord
Grant me the wisdom of the mind of man,
But keep within me the heart of a child.

LAUGHTER

At nine and a half
Though claiming 'nearly ten',
In a boating pool in Rhyl,
I learned a lesson about friendship,
About a certain kind of laughter
And something about boats and water.
I learned how to row
And caught several crabs;
Discovered the consequence
Of balancing with one foot on land
And the other in a boat.

That was when they laughed,
As I stood in the mud,
Grey flannel shorts wet and clinging,
Sodden socks that squelched beneath my toes
And a face crimson with shame.

I heard their laughter,
Or at least a noise that sounded like laughter.
A noise that mocked and jeered
And fell upon my ears
With the strength of blows.
Yet, amid the guffaws and cackles of derision,
One face looked down with nine year old concern,
One hand reached out to help me up the bank,
And then he smiled the smile of a friend
The rueful smile that said,
'Hard luck.'

I have heard, since then,
So much laughter,
Seen so many smiles;
Scornful laughs, sarcastic smiles,
Titters, sniggers and snorts,
Heads thrown back in sheer delight,
Tears of joy
And the honest open laughter
Of those who saw the funny side of themselves.
But of all the hoots and giggles
I doubt if I shall ever see
A smile more welcome
Than the grin that said,
'Whatever happens, I am your friend.'

Lord
As I speak and listen
Let me not laugh at another's expense,
Or smile at innuendo of gossip or malice.
Let me never misuse my sense of humour.
Let me be loyal to friends even in laughter.
Humour is a gift,
A kind of safety valve;
Let me use it wisely.
Let all my laughing and joking
Be open and kind and grateful.

WHO IS LISTENING?

I saw two people walking,
Talking with great animation,
Both of them speaking at the same time.
Could they hear each other,
Or were they just talking and not listening?
Would one say tomorrow,
'But I *told* you, yesterday,'
And the other reply,
'Did you? I don't remember that.'

Beneath the chatter and the flow of clichés
About the weather,
The football and last night's TV,
Are people saying things
That I do not want to hear?
Beneath the banter of lunchtime,
Are cries for help drowned in the coffee?
Is there a scream I cannot hear
Behind the tired smiles
And the shouts of
'See you in the morning'?

Friends talk, without hearing.
Committees talk, and no one listens.
Families talk, and no one pays attention.
The lonely weep, but their neighbours are deaf.
In the High Street
God himself speaks of his love.
Every day he offers eternal life
But his voice is lost
In the roar of the traffic.

Lord
Forgive me
That I choose not to hear
The voices that disturb me.
Help me to hear when someone sighs,
To notice a face, see the eyes
To be aware, to be sensitive
To the silent shout of a friend in need.
Teach me
To hear *between* the words.
Open my inward ear
So that I will hear your voice
When you speak to me.
Remind me, again and again,
That you are always listening.

THERE BUT FOR THE GRACE OF GOD . . .

In the news today
There will be stories of people in trouble,
People who have met failure
At some point in their lives,
And we who hear and read
Will make judgements.
It is so easy for me
To shake my head in disapproval
When I have not had the same temptations
Or met the same problems.
Who am I to judge another?
I do not know
What pressures, what suffering,
Others have had to face.
But I do know
That there is a hair's breadth
Between success and failure.

Deep down I know
That there, but for the grace of God, go I.

Lord
Today, if I hear something
About a friend or colleague,
Prevent me from making a judgement that is
    unkind.
If I read in the paper
About the mistakes of a fellow man or woman,
Do not let my mind turn to gossip.
Help me to see the best in people,
To hate the sin but love the sinner;
For there is no one who is beyond redemption,
Or beyond your love;
And when I hear opinions,
May I remember that they are *only* opinions,
For only you know the truth.

Lord, you have taught us
That love is patient and kind,
That love is never pleased
When others make mistakes;
But love looks for and rejoices in goodness.
Love does not want to expose faults.
Love always believes the best;
For love is always hopeful, always patient,
Love never gives up.
Teach me Lord
To make all my judgements
In the light of the love that never dies.

DREAMING

Daydreamer, where are you?
Your eyes are open
But focused on another world.
Your face is before me
But your mind is somewhere else,
Dreaming. Dreaming.
I do not know where your thoughts are,
But I know how the journey is made
For I am a fellow traveller
On the paths that lead to dreams.

Sometimes it's an escape,
A flight to happier times,
A visit to the past
Where memory has erased
All that was regrettable or sad
And preserved only laughter and happiness,
For memory is a comfort, a blessing

Where all the love, the conversation,
The days of sunshine
Are waiting to be re-lived.
Memory is a treasure store,
A casket to be opened with joy,
My own version of the truth
As it seems to me.

Or is it fantasy that I fly to?
Do the things I long for
Become reality in my mind?
Am I on a trip to the place
Where imagination rules,
Where what might be, is?
Building castles, sailing seas,
Making speeches in my head?
Have I inherited a fortune,
Won thousands of pounds on Premium Bonds,
Distributing with largess to family and friends,
Buying cottages with roses round the door?
Or do I dream of the attainable,
Of what work and thrift
And love and care might bring,
Of all I could give or share
With the people in my life?
For then 'dream' is another word for hope.

Lord
I am grateful for the dreams of memory,
For the wealth of good things remembered,
The source of comfort when days are lean.

I rejoice in the ability you have given
To live in worlds beyond my reach.
But this day turn my dreams to prayer,
To living hope
That the day will be blessed
With dreams that come true.
May this day be a good day.
May every smile be returned.
May conversation be without malice.
May my work be worthy of the gifts
You have given me.
May my friends be happy.
May the sorrowful be comforted.
May the hungry be fed.
May my sins be forgiven
So that I may rest in peace
To dream again.

THE FEAR OF LOVE

So many serious faces
In the shops and walking down the street,
Unsmiling, tight mouths,
An insular people
With secret thoughts, in secret minds,
Imprisoned, waiting to be released.
And the key that unlocks the warmth of humanity
Is as simple as a greeting or a smile.

I see my reflection in a window
And I wonder
Why am I so shut up within myself,
So withdrawn?
Am I afraid of other people,
Afraid to smile, afraid to talk?
Have I forgotten, or did I ever know
How to rejoice in simply being alive?

When people meet and exchange pleasantries,
The joy of their meeting
Stays with them for minutes after,
And then slowly
The shutters fall once again.

People who live in the same street
Do not know each other, do not speak.
People travel on the same train
In the same compartment,
Month after month, year after year,
And they could be in different countries.

If I cannot care and share
With those close to me,
How can I care for those who are far off?
Do I have some responsibility for the fact
That one half of the world
Suspects the other half?

Dear Lord
Forgive me for being afraid to love,
For being a miser,
Hoarding to myself the most precious gift I possess.
You did not fear to give your love,
To give and give again
Until there was nothing left to give
But your life.
Forgive me if I am afraid
To give a little time,
A little laughter, a little joy.
I am afraid of love
Because loving is giving
And I am afraid of the cost.
Lord, fill me with your love
So that I might share
The surplus of your riches.

TRAVELLING

Suitcase locked, pockets checked,
Keys, money,
Cheque book, credit cards, tickets.
Did I remember my tooth-brush?
Did I pack the book I'm reading?
Where did I put the asprins?
Time to leave.
Trains and planes and buses
Will not wait for my tooth-brush.
(I needed a new one anyway.)
'Cheerio mum.'
'Yes, I'll be careful.'
'I'll write.'
'I'll phone.'
'Bye-bye son, look after mummy for me.'
'Good-bye darling.'

There was a time
When a fourpenny bus ride to New Brighton
Was an adventure,
A ferry boat crossing of the Mersey river
An epic voyage to a distant land.
But now,
Fifty miles, a hundred, two hundred,
Is taken in a stride.
All the world seems to be on the move;
The air is heavy with after-shave
From faces glowing
Over pin-stripe suits and 'executive' cases.
Tweeds and twinsets tow cases on wheels,
And we wonder if those we love
Will look older.

Lord
You exist beyond the space we cannot cross,
Beyond the stars and planets,
And yet
There is no voyage made
Where you are not a fellow-traveller.
In all our journeys,
When we are weary, strengthen us,
When we are afraid, comfort us,
When we feel alone may we know your closeness.
At the end of the day
May we be united with those we love
And with you
Who are Alpha and Omega,
Life's beginning and journey's end.

CHRISTMAS LOVE

Once again
There is excitement in the air,
Holly and mistletoe,
Christmas trees, fairy lights,
And cards from forgotten friends.
Streets and shops possess a different feeling.

At this time of year
People seem to be laughing and talking
In grocers and department stores;
And everywhere there are carols.
For a brief week or so
There is love in the air,
Gaiety and warmth,
And all because of a child
Born long ago.

At this time of year
We are more generous,
We spend on gifts,
We make an effort to see family and friends.
We talk together,
Sing together, eat together,
Savouring the intangible wonder of Christmas.

Lord, at this time
Help me to spread my generosity
A little further,
Not necessarily with money
But with time and love.
You gave yourself
To the world for eternity,
Help me to give a little of myself,
If only for an hour,
To a neighbour who is alone.
Let me give a gift to a child in need.
Help me to let the love that is in my family
Overflow wherever it can.

Show me the ways in which I may share
The spirit of Christmas love.

As a child I wished
That it could be Christmas every day,
And grown-ups laughed;
But the love that came at Christmas
Is with us every day.
Lord I know I can be generous
With my love and time in this season,
So may your gift to me
Be Christmas love
That I can share
In every day of every season.

A LOVING WAY OF LIVING

In less time than it takes
For me to get to work,
In three quarters of an hour,
An aircraft can fly from England to America.
It seems beyond belief
And yet, we're told it's true,
A fighter that's faster
Than the missiles it fires.
We are living in an age of miracles,
Of jets and satellites, of rockets to the moon,
Of silicon chips, of computers and robots.
In my living room I can choose,
At the touch of a button,
Entertainment in living colour
Or international news of conflict and hunger
That shows we have not changed since Adam.

Throughout the centuries
We have not changed.
Our nature, our tempers, our passions
Are just the same.
Oh, we are clever in the things we can do.
Our hands and minds are skilful
In harnessing the energy of the universe,
But we have not changed.

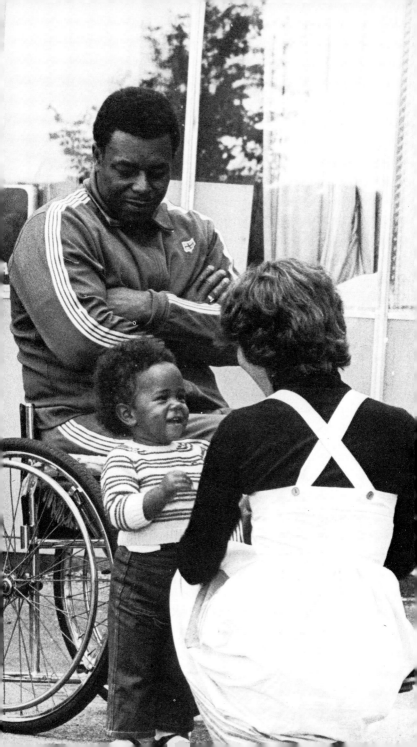

When men were covered in woad
And made their homes in caves,
Did they envy?
Were they jealous?
Did they steal or cheat or fight?
Where did they differ from those who live
In the semi-detached caves of suburbia?

Lord
You have given us immense power and freedom,
Above all
The power and the freedom
To choose or reject love.
Help me to choose
A loving way of living,
For only love can change
The things that matter.
Only love can change people
For love is at the heart of creation.
Love is of God.
God is love.

MORNING LIGHT

Looking through a window
With sleepy morning eyes
I saw an artist at work.
The early light
Tingeing sky pink and rose
Struggled through mist and cloud
And bathed my mundane view in mystery.
Rooftops glistening, wet with morning dew
Glowed with brief reflected glory.
In the miracle of morning
Back garden sheds,
Victorian bricks and sash windows
Are dressed in borrowed finery;
A precious gift from the rising winter sun,
A fleeting prize that must be captured
Before the greyness over-rules.

Beneath the rafters of every suburban house
Alarm clocks rattle, kettles boil
And razors fight their endless battle
With bearded chins,
Unaware of unheralded majesty
Passing silent overhead.
Days begin with breakfast
And the Lord of life
Waits without acknowledgement.

Lord of the heavens
Your light transforms
The skylines of cities and towns.
Forgive me for those days
In which the morning paper
And the wireless news
Take precedence over you.
Each and every day
You offer me the miracle of your presence,
The treasure of your love,
A loving presence
That can transform my life
If only I could be still
For long enough to receive your gift.
Lord, each morning,
Open my eyes
And let me live
In the light of your love.

WISE MEN

Wise men looking for a king
Were shown an aspect of a vunerable God.
Clothed in swaddling, love slept in a manger,
A simplicity which puzzles the wisdom
Of every generation;
For the personality of Jesus is not simple.
We cannot pin him down,
We cannot isolate him,
Pigeon-hole him,
Define him.

Gentle Jesus, meek and mild,
Stands beside
Jesus revolutionary,
Liberator,
Healer,
Priest,
King,
And brother of the poor and oppressed.
Jesus lives,
Not between the covers of theological volumes,
But wherever men and women gather in his name.

He cannot be confined to sanctuaries,
Churches or cathedrals;
He does not belong to political parties,
Yet he belongs to all who need him.
His wisdom is not our wisdom.
His love cannot be measured by our minds.
Yet his love is always within our reach.
Jesus said,
Come to me all you
Who are heavy laden,
With anxiety
With fear
With poverty
With sickness
With pain
With grief
And I will give you rest.

Dear Lord
Philosophers, theologians,
The wise men of centuries
Have tried to fathom
The depths of your being,
And in my small way
I have used the gifts you have given me
To explore your love.
Forgive me for the times
When intellectual pride
Has prevented my coming close to you.
Forgive me for allowing my cleverness
To come between my needs and your love.

Forgive me for the times
When I have confused others
With the artfulness of my own words.
Lord, give me true simplicity,
Openness of mind and heart.
Remove the scales
That I have allowed to grow
Over my inward ear and eye.
Help me to see and hear
Your wisdom and your love.

LORD
of the
evening

May every day
Begin with space
Enough to see
My saviour's face.

May every hour
Possess within it
The space to live
A prayerful minute.

And may I find,
From night's alarms,
The space between
My saviour's arms.

Aylesford Priory Retreat

PATIENCE

I wish I had more patience
I'm always wanting things, now,
Wishing for things to happen now.
It isn't easy to be patient
When every day I pass a huge poster
Saying 'Why wait? Buy it now!'
I suppose I live in a society
That demands *instant* satisfaction.
'Have it today' with easy payments, credit cards
And hire purchase.
But I can't blame society.
Society is me and my friends.

When I was a child
Part of the spice of life was waiting for things.
Waiting for a bike, a watch,
Waiting for Saturday, when at last
I had saved enough pocket money
To buy that penknife.

Waiting was a pleasure that could be savoured.
Now, waiting is an irritation.
My patience is short
When things don't happen soon enough.
I even expect my prayers to be answered *instantly*.

Lord help me to be patient
Not only in wanting things
But help me to be patient with people.
Help me to be patient with my wife and children.
Each day, each hour, each minute,
Help me to breathe slowly, to listen and to wait.
Help me to be patient with myself,
And not least, to wait patiently for your guidance
This night and always.

STARS

Tonight the sky is calm
With the still, cool light of stars,
And yet they are not silent.
On such a night
The heavens salute their creator
With shouts of joy
Too exquisite for the human ear.
Tonight is a festival.
Virtuoso performers take their places
Form dazzling patterns
Brilliant clusters
And they are perfect.

And I have known them
These stars
From the days of my childhood
To the days of my children.
Walking down country lanes
We have identified the Plough
Pointed to the Pole
And felt small beneath their majesty.

On such a night I have held the North Star
Between the mainmast shrouds of a tall ship
Steering for home.
Ageless mariners have looked
To that constant star
And are looking, tonight.

Tonight, each star and planet
Is the splash of a sounding
Measuring the depth of the Almighty.
Tonight there is so much laughter in the sky
Because you have filled it with old friends
Holding lanterns
And singing songs of love across the heavens.
And once again I know
That your light is ever before me.

BEDTIME

In this evening hour
In the last minutes
Of a long day
I am grateful for the joy
Of clean sheets and a pillow,
For the prospect
Of seven or eight hours
Of physical rest,
For the pleasure of closing my eyes.
Lord of the evening
Thank you for the night,
For my bed
And for sleep.

So often bedtime is simply a gap
Between days.
A habit, a necessary interruption
When really
It is yet another gift
That I take for granted.
To lie in bed is luxury.
Here, between the sheets,
Beneath my eyelids
The trials of today
Sink into my subconscious
And become history.

Lord of the night
Thank you for the rest
That each sunset brings,
For the peace and quietness
Of late hours,
For the stillness
Of the stars and the night.
And may those who cannot sleep
Know the comfort of your presence.

Lord help me to enjoy
The gift of evening,
Let me not relive the tensions
Of the day that has gone;
Prevent me from fighting tomorrow's battles
Before tomorrow's dawn.
Let me savour this space.
Let me be conscious of these untroubled
Minutes and seconds.
Let me be refreshed.
Let me rest mind and body.
Let me place my trust
In you, who have led me
To this time and place,
In you, the giver of life and light
And sleep.

MISTAKES

Lord of the evening
Someone let me down today.
I was upset and said harsh things.
It's so easy to be superior
When other people make mistakes,
To wag the finger, shake the head,
As if I had never made a mistake,
Never let anyone down.
And if I concede that there are times
When I am less than perfect,
I expect other people to be understanding
To be sympathetic, kind, merciful.

Lord of the evening
Forgive me
For my lack of understanding.

Lord, when I have made mistakes
I hope that they will soon be forgotten,
That people will behave
As if they never happened.
I don't want to feel the flush of guilt
That comes whenever my errors
Are brought into the open.
Yet so often I am less than kind
To those who have offended me.

Lord, help me to show the same mercy to others
That I would wish for myself.
Lord, preserve me
From any desire for revenge.
Stop me from ever trying
To get my own back.
You taught hard lessons
When you told us to 'turn the other cheek',
'Love your enemies', 'go the extra mile'.
So often I have been your enemy
Because of my unkindness
My selfishness
My lack of love.
Yet I know that you still love me,
That there is no end to your mercy.
Loving, patient, suffering Lord,
Help me to give to others
The forgiving love I continually receive from you.

LOOKING FOR PEACE

In quietness I sometimes realise
How much I need noise.
In quietness I sometimes see
The peace that belongs
To a lively household
Full of people.
So often
I've searched for peace
Longed for peace
And in my search confused 'peace'
With being alone or being still.
Finding quietness and tranquility
Is easy, they are just places,
But peace is in the mind.

So I ask myself, what are
The moments of real peace of mind
That I have known,
And I find that I have been at peace
In laughter, in real genuine laughter.
And laughter shared is even better.
At mealtimes
In conversation with friends round a table
There are moments of mutual peace.
Life is not so difficult
When you talk about it
With a knife and a fork in your hand.

And work
In work there can be peace,
Problems recede, even disappear
In the concentration
Of doing some job well.

In prayer
When I view my problems
Held up in relief against eternity
Peace begins.
In prayer
When I realise that there is no need
For words
There is the peace
That passes my understanding.

I have looked to distant dreams
For peace,
But your peace
Is in the commonplace
In the daily round.
Lord help me to find and enjoy
The peace that lives
In laughter
In conversation
In friendship
In family
In work
And in prayer.

Lord of the evening
May I always remember
That the knowledge of your love
Is the touch of peace
And that nothing is beyond your reach.

SLEEP ON IT

Here I am
At the end of another day
With so many things I should have done,
Not done.
There are letters I should have written
People I should have talked to
Work I should have started
And work I should have finished.
Unanswered family questions
About the children
Their progress at school
Their choice of career.
Personal questions
Where do I stand?
What is my next step?
And suddenly night has fallen
And the streets are still.

But what am I asking?
It would be a strange day
In which all work was finished.
All questions answered
All decisions made.
There wouldn't be much to live for.

To be alive
Is to work
To make efforts
To ask questions.
Living needs contrasts, opposites.
If there is no work there is no rest.
Without questions there are no answers.
All laughter and no tears
Would be nonsense.
Failure enriches success.
Why should I think that this day
Has been any less fulfilled than others?
Every day is incomplete,
Every day leaves something for tomorrow,
That's what tomorrow is for.

Lord of the night
Be with me through the hours of darkness,
Let all my questions,
Problems, decisions,
Be enveloped in sleep
That through the mystery
Of the sleeping mind
The difficulties of this day
Will be seen to be easier
In the morning light.
Into your hands O Lord,
I commit my spirit.

THE GIFT OF VISION

Lord, in these few moments
Before sleep
I wish there was more time
To think things over.
But how long do I need
When it only takes a few seconds
To travel a long way in thought?
In a few seconds
I can recapture the peace
That has been stored in my mind
Over years.
In the twinkle of an eye
I can see mountains and lakes,
Sanctuaries of peace in my head.

Even in the bustle
Of my everyday work
It is possible to retreat
For a brief instant
To the peace that I have known
And that still exists.

Lord you have given us
The gift of vision,
The ability to look beyond
The difficulties that surround us,
Help me to use that vision
To be able to stand back
From immediate problems
To see them against the immensity of time.
For against a vision like that
My problems begin to look small.

Lord of life
Help me to recognise the moments
That are given to me each day,
Moments of stillness
That can bring me into your presence,
Moments that glimpse eternity
Through the flickering seconds.
Let me see the peace that exists
In the eye of the storm.
Peace in the midst of activity.
Let me have that vision
In which questions and problems
Are lost in the vastness
Of the endless love
That surrounds me
This night and always.

FACING THE TRUTH

In this evening light
In my head
I can hear the words
Spoken today
Which hurt me.
They were unkind and probably meant to hurt.
My first reaction was to hit back
But when I think about it
Perhaps what hurt most
What made the remark sting
Was the element of truth in it.
And I suppose the fact is
I don't like being told the truth
About myself.

'Oh that God would give us
Eyes to see ourselves
As others see us.'
I would not really like that.
When I think about myself
I don't like to think about my failings.

I'm inclined to keep counting my qualities
To justify myself
To consider the flaws in my character
As minor blemishes.
The last thing I want
Is to see my faults
Nor do I want somebody else pointing at my sins.
So I am angry and hit back
Because the truth hurts.

Lord of the evening
In your presence
I can hide nothing.
You know me as I am
Inside and out.
Before you I am humbled
But not angry.
Why?
Is it because I know
That you will go on loving me
In spite of my weakness?

Lord, help me to listen
To criticism of myself
So that I might face the truth
And learn.
Help me to see the faults of my friends
With understanding,
To forgive,
And to go on loving
As you do.

A SMILE

Lord of the evening
There are some people
Who always make me feel better
For meeting them.
The people who make me smile.
They have a warmth about them, an inner gaiety.

After a few minutes in their company
The world seems a better place.
Somehow, my problems and difficulties
Are not nearly so bad.
What gift is it that such people have?
What is the secret of their infectious joy?

Lord I'm thinking about a particular friend
Who always makes me feel good.
Why is it that I am always lifted up
Simply by the presence of that friend?
I know that to give out warmth and joy
Is impossible without love.
Such a person has to have a loving, caring spirit.
Is it that they care more about people than things?
Is it that for the few minutes they are with me
I catch a glimpse of love at work?

Lord
Tomorrow I will meet a number of people
And I would like them to feel better
For having spent some time with me.
It will mean that I will have to think
More about them than myself
And that won't be easy,
It will take effort.
But of all the things
That I could spend my energy on
Few things could have more value
Than making someone smile
Or feel a little love.
Lord, help me to bring some joy or warmth
Into every meeting.

THE EMPTY HOUSE

Tonight I feel slightly lost,
Isolated, in need of company.
I always feel like this
When my family are away
Even for a few days.
My life feels empty
The house feels deserted
Just a house not a home.
The days seem to drag on
And I long for the return
Of voices, noise, laughter,
And I wonder how I would manage
If I was always alone.

Lord of the evening
Loneliness isn't just solitude
Or lack of company,
I have felt lonely
Even in the midst of my family
A deep aching void inside me,
Times when I have been unable to share
Worries, questions, guilt.
Times when my voice makes the right responses
My feet are firm on my own hearth-rug
But my mind is adrift,
Alone on a sea of anxieties.
Lord at these times
I seem to lose touch with my friends
And you.

In this particular evening reflection
I know that I am never really alone
But Lord, I need the assurance
That you are present with me
In my darkest moment,
That I do not have to seek you
Because you are always beside me.
Make your presence real for me
In all places and at all times
Pour your spirit
Of comfort and strength
Into every lonely mind, including mine.

Lord of the evening
Into your hands I commend my spirit.

I AM NOT WORTHY

This night
In your presence Lord
I lay the burden of my doubts
All unanswered questions
All the problems of my conscience
The wrongs that I have done to others
The guilt of things neglected;
The pain of cruel words
The stupidity of my pride and vanity
The arrogance and conceit of my selfishness
My little faith, my lack of love.

Lord I am not worthy to be in your presence
Say but the word and I shall be healed.

Lord this night
In your presence
I look for forgiveness,
I look for help.
Help me to love;
Help me to serve;
Help me to suffer;
Help me to trust;
Help me to live.
May your forgiving love
Live in me,
That it might no longer be I that live
But you who live in me.

The Lord said,
Come to me
All you that are heavy laden
And I will give you rest.

I will not leave you desolate.
I will come to you.

In that day you will know that I am in my father and you
in me, and I in you.

Lord, your love is too great
For me to understand.
Grant me a quiet night
And a perfect end.

COMFORT THE SORROWFUL

Lord of the evening
Today I received a letter
About a friend who has lost her husband.
She is distressed,
Confused, numbed
By grief.
Her world seems to have ended
And no-one feels able to help.
Nobody can reach her.

Her sorrow imprisons her
Like a stone wall.
Loving Lord
Show me how to help her.

So often I am embarrassed
By grief.
I don't know what to say
Or what to do;
And the easiest thing
Is to do nothing.
If I write it is so hard
To find the right words;
If I visit I feel at a loss
Uncomfortable
In the silence of sorrow.
Lord help me to make an attempt to comfort
Even if my efforts are stumbling
And inadequate.

Lord
Grief cannot be erased by magic.
But what would comfort me?
Perhaps the knowledge
That for the one I love
Suffering has ended.
I would like to be reminded
Of the promises of Chirst,
That he has gone
To prepare a place for us
So that where he is we shall be.

To be reminded that
The eye has not seen
Nor the ear heard
Nor has it entered the heart of man
What things have been prepared
For those that love God;
And that nothing
Can separate us from the love of Christ
Not even death.

Lord
In the presence of sorrow
Give me the courage
To share my faith.

MASKS

At the end of the day
I sometimes wonder if I have met anyone.
I mean *really* met.
Sometimes I think I have spent the day
Talking to images, façades, masks,
But never the person behind the eyes.

We all wear masks,
A different face for the boss
The bank manager
A friend.
I suppose masks
Can be good things,
Protective, reassuring,
But they do prevent meeting.
I know that if
I want to really meet someone,
I have to have the courage
To let my own mask fall.

If I am to know a friend,
My children,
Perhaps especially
If I am to know my wife,
We must be able to face each other
Without masks.

196

Lord of the night,
You know me
No matter what mask or façade
I may be showing to the world.
There is no way
That I can hide from you.
You know my weakness
And my strength
Better than I know myself.
Each day Lord,
Help me to be open and receptive
To those who need my friendship.
Help me not to hide
From those who need my love.
So that when I come before you
With nothing to conceal
What I am or what I have done,
I may dare to look
At the love in your face.

Lord of the evening, help me.

ALL MY TOMORROWS

Lord of the evening
The day has come to rest
And in the quiet, I am at peace.
I wish this calmness
Could stay with me
Throughout the working day.
Yet so often
I am irritable at the start of a day.
I wonder why?
I suppose there are physical reasons,
A natural reluctance
To leave the warmth and security
Of sleep;
And perhaps a deep-seated
Unwillingness to face the tasks
That await me.
Yet in any working day
The hours I spend with my family
Are so few
I can't afford to spoil any of them.

Lord
I know that when tomorrow begins
The things I say and do
Will create 'moods'
That will affect me and others
For hours.
One sharp word from me
Could mean that two or three
Other people will start
Off on the wrong foot.
It can make a difference
To so many things.

Lord
May I know the peace of your presence
When daylight breaks.
Tomorrow, help me to think before I speak
Help me to realise that I am not the only person
Who finds it difficult to start the day.
Let me know that your peace is present
Not only in the stillness of the night
But that in the midst
Of all the activities of the day.
I have only to breathe your name
To know your peace.
Help me to remember that
Now and always.

SONS AND DAUGHTERS

Tonight
I'm thinking about my children.
They're almost grown up now,
In their teens.
The eldest already has the vote
Is part of the electorate.
When I speak to one of my sons
On the telephone
I'm surprised to hear
A young man's voice.
Are these the children
Who squealed with delight
As we splashed at the sea-shore?
Who asked me
'Why did God make wasps?'
And
'Daddy, what was it like in the olden days?'

And now they are talking and thinking
About careers and jobs
Each with their secret hopes and dreams,
And it seems like only yesterday
That I stood in their place
And wondered about the future.
Yet *I* still have hopes and dreams
So what can I advise them?
That life is a continous exploration
An ongoing search for the dream,
That life is not a job or a qualification
Or a particular success,
But a series of discoveries.

Lord
How can I tell them
That even when they are pensioners
They will still be on the nursery slopes
Of discovery,
That the excitement of being alive
Is not arriving at destinations
Or achieving goals
But making the journey.
How can I convey to them
That they must never stop searching,
That if they do
They will have stopped living.

Lord help me in my life
To share with my children
The joy and the pain
Of the search.

I'M SORRY

I heard a man and a woman
Arguing in the street tonight.

Lord of the evening
Why is it so hard to say
I'm sorry?

Every day, homes are left in anger,
Front doors slammed,
Engines revved fiercely
Because of a few sharp, tetchy words,
Voices are raised about stupid, silly matters
And before we know where we are
People have parted.

Lord, it happens to me,
I don't want it to happen.

I don't ever want to leave in anger.
Even as the door shuts behind me
I ache with the stupidity of my own actions.
It takes just a few neurotic seconds
To create an atmosphere
That could take hours or years
To recover from.
It could all be over in seconds,
A quick hug, the words 'I'm sorry'.
But 'I'm sorry' is so hard to say.

Lord
Why is it so difficult
To make peace with each other?
No wonder there are wars.
Is it pride that holds my mouth tight,
A childish feeling
That I am not the one who should apologise?
It wasn't my fault?
In these flare-ups
What does it matter *whose* fault it is?
The only thing that matters is love and harmony.
Lord turning my back in anger is weakness,
It reduces me as a human being.
Give me the courage,
The stature,
To say, 'I'm sorry'.

. . . And may those two people
I heard in the street
End this day in mutual forgiveness.

EYES TO SEE

The setting sun is silent
Yet it tells its own story.
Before I see it again
That same sun will have shined
On vast continents,
Warmed rich and poor,
Made shadows on mountains,
Islands, jungles, cities.

And here I am
In the last of the day's light.
What can I see?
Just another day ended
Or thousands greeting a new day
In other lands?

In the waking light of my new day,
With toast and marmalade
And a cup of tea,
What will I see?
A hasty snack before the morning rush?
Or will there be on my table
Oranges from Spain,
Leaves from India,
Bread from the wheatfields
Of English Downs,
A humble breakfast or a feast?
Lord, give me eyes to see
In the light you shed upon the world.

Lord, let me see the magic
Of common place things.
Let me see the mystery of creation in the sky
That goes on being endless
Day after day.
Let me see the wonder of creation
In the families of birds
That have flown for thousands of years
Across endless miles of sea,
Guided by what?

Let me see the whole of creation
In a blade of grass
And the reason for it all
In an act of kindness.

Lord of the evening, open my eyes,
So that this night
Shall not be empty
But full of the knowledge of you.

A QUIET MIND

Tonight
I've had a curious thought,
It's a paradox,
The more I seek for a quiet mind
The more anxious I seem to become.
The more I examine my conscience
The more disturbed I become.
The more I try to plan the future
The more worried I become.
It's a simple rule really,
Anxiety breeds anxiety.

Lord, it cannot be wrong
To want a quiet mind
Or a bad thing to try
To clear my conscience.

And sometimes tomorrow
Has to be planned today.
Perhaps I try too hard,
Perhaps I do too much
Planning, and examining.
Perhaps I spend too much time
Thinking about the state I'm in,
Perhaps the real trouble
Is that I worry too much about me.

The times I have found peace
Are those times when
My mind has centred on something
Outside of myself,
Listening to somebody else's story,
Thinking about an idea in a book.
I have found contentment in physical work.
In fact on all those occasions
When I have been 'lost'
In something other than me.

Lord, this night
Help me to die to self,
So that I might awake
To live more fully
For others and in you.
Help me to trust
That as you have led me this far
Your guidance will continue.

THE CHILD AND THE FATHER

Lord of the evening
Here I am again
Like a child
Who needs comfort and reassurance.
Lord, I keep coming to you
With regrets.
I keep asking you to do things for me.
As a parent I know that I cannot always
Do everything for my children,
I know that they have to stand
On their own feet.
Perhaps the best thing
That I can offer my children
Is the love that assures them
That no matter what happens
They can always come home.

Right now I need the assurance
Of that kind of love,
That you will be standing by me
When things go right
And when things go wrong.
I often wonder if my children
Believe me.
I wonder if they ever feel
That some problem simply
Cannot be shared with me,
I wonder if they really trust me.
Trusting is difficult,
Yet without trust
There can be no peace of mind.

Lord in the days that lie before me
Help me to trust in your loving presence;
In the knowledge
That at the end of every day
I can come to you
As a child to a father.

Lord of the evening,
Heavenly Father,
Hear my prayer.

COURAGE FOR THE NIGHT

Lord of the evening
The day has passed
But the day's problems are still with me.
Sometimes I wish the day away,
I long for the night,
Hoping that sleep
Will envelop my difficulties,
Banish them forever
Beneath the blanket of darkness;
That I might rise to a fresh, new day
With my slate wiped clean.
But day follows day
And I am still the same person
With the same problems, questions, difficulties.

Lord, I wish I could stand at a distance,
Far away from today,
Then perhaps I could smile
At today's problems.
If I look at last year's worries
Or even last month's
I know for a fact that I survived,
And that gives me hope.
But I don't want to run away
Or live my life at a distance,
I want to enjoy
The daily battle of life
As I live it.

Tonight Lord,
Give me courage
To see tomorrow as a friend,
As a new opportunity to put things right,
To see the new day as a gift,
My millionth chance to start again,
To see that the new day
Is rich in possibilities,
That even the wildest dreams
Can come true
Where there is faith, hope and love.

Lord, fill my dreams tonight
With your spirit
So that I might face the world
Armed with these gifts
That nothing can destroy.

THE HOPE OF HIS COMING

Here I wait in quiet hope
That you will come
To water my barren fields,
To make blossom the flower and fruit
That wither in merciless heat.
Do not forsake me.

I am the earth
On which large eyed children thirst and die.
I am the crusted soil
Watered by the tears
Of mothers, fathers, sons and daughters.
Hear my cry,
Father, I thirst.

Here I wait in quiet hope
That you will come
To open the door to release me,
For I am a prisoner.
Here I sit, in many places,
In prisons political and criminal.
In labour camp, in hospital,
In the high-rise flat,
In a bed-sitting room.
Imprisoned by my brother.
Hear me when I call,
And come to me.
Now is the time of your coming
Do not pass me by.

Here I wait in quiet hope
That you will come
To possess my being,
To inhabit me,
For I have no strength left,
No power to lift myself,
Every sinew, every bone
Fast bound by selfishness,

Grasping at life
There is nothing my hands can hold
Nothing preserve.
I can struggle no more,
Defeated, defenceless, exhausted.
So Lord,
Here I wait in quiet hope
That you will come.

Save us Lord, while we are awake;
Protect us while we sleep;
That we may keep watch with Christ
And rest with him in peace.

BEFORE I SLEEP

Lord, before I sleep
Help me to share with you
The things I am anxious about,
For I am anxious about many things;
About my family,
About relationships with people,
About the future.
I am anxious about security;
Money in the bank,
A pension, income-tax returns,
Rates, a roof over our heads,
Clothes on our backs,
Food in the larder.

And the Lord said,
Be not anxious about your life, what you shall eat, nor

about your body, what you shall wear, for life is more
than food and the body more than clothing. Which of
you by being anxious can add a cubit to his span of life?
Your father knows that you need these things. Instead
seek his Kingdom and all these things shall be yours as
well.

Lord, before I sleep
Help me to remember with gratitude
All the blessings of my life;
For the home into which I was born,
For the friends that I grew up with
In school and afterwards,
Help me to be grateful for companionship,
For laughter, and family love.
Help me to be worthy of your trust,
To be grateful for the people
You have given me to love.
For your endless grace to me,
For in seeing your goodness
I am lifed above the troubles of the day-to-day.
Give me a grateful mind,
A mind aware of the love that is poured out,
Given freely,
Even to the least deserving.

And the Lord said through his apostle Paul,
Let your requests be made known to God;
And the peace of God
Which passes all understanding
Will keep your heart and mind in Christ.

Lord, before I sleep
Help me to see
What is important and what is not.
Show me the secret
That enabled Paul to be content
In any situation.
Help me to give into your care,
My life, my talents, my time.
Help me to know the strength and peace
That comes to those
Who totally submit their lives
To Christ.
In spite of my failings,
My self-will, my arrogance,
My pride, my ambitions.
Take my life Lord, in spite of me,
In spite of my own self-deceit.
Take my life and let it be
Consecrated, Lord, to thee.

Father,
The moment I lift my eyes towards you
I move from the darkness of self
Into the light of your love.
The brightness
Of your goodness and love
Melts away anxieties,
Like morning sun on the mist of night.
The warmth of that light upon my brow
Brings, beyond understanding,
Peace, like summer sun.

And the breeze on my face
Is the kiss of your spirit.

Lord,
Help me to be quiet and still
In the peace of your presence
This night and always.

CHRISTMAS EVE

On this special night,
I am thinking about children.
Since the day began
Thousands of children have been born,
In hospitals, homes, shanty towns,
Children who have opened their eyes
For the first time.
Even at this moment,
Somewhere, a child
Is drawing its first breath in total innocence.
There is something of a mystery about babies,
Especially at Christmas time.

A child,
Wide, open-eyed trusting infant
Who draws love from me, and returns it.
There is hope in the *fact*
Of the newly born;
So much potential for love.
When I look at a baby
Who holds my finger
In a tiny gentle grip,
I find it hard to imagine
That I was once a child.

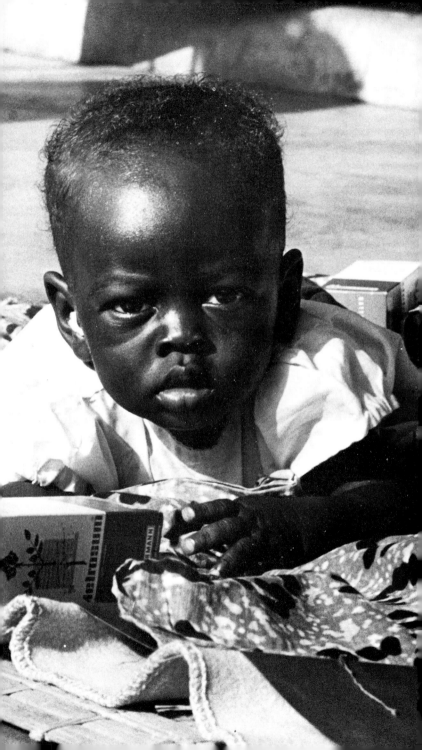

Did I have so much potential for love?
What happened to that child
That made hardness, suspicion,
Envy and malice, grow?
Did simplicity have to die?

Soon on Christmas Day,
People will sing and rejoice,
Children will laugh and play
In celebration of the birth of a child
Whose name became love.

Lord of this special night
Help me to protect innocence
Wherever I see it.
Help me not to abuse the simplicity of children
Who look to me to learn.
Help me to nurture love and truth;
And let the love and truth
That was born in a stable so long ago,
Be born again in me tonight.

THE INSTRUMENTS OF PEACE

This meditation was written when the author was a university chaplain. It was later broadcast in the BBC programme 'Lighten our Darkness'.

Cold and shivering we stood
Around the Ditchling Beacon,
High on Sussex Downs,
Sussex students and chaplain
Not much older,
Sipping soup from steaming flasks
As rosey girls unpacked sandwiches
And waited for the dawn.

In the first light
We gave thanks for the night long trek
With the singing of the hymn,
Dear Lord and Father of Mankind
Forgive our Foolish Ways.
We sang and rubbed our itching eyes.
No one saw the flight begin
But there, in the centre of our circle,
A lark had risen, as if from the midst of us;
And soaring higher and higher
Surprised us with his voice.

A tiny bird bursting with song
That filled our eyes with joy,
Our ears with his thrill
And printed on our memories
A moment of peace
That soothes me still.
And so we sang,

Drop thy still dews of quietness
Till all our strivings cease;
Take from our souls the strain and stress
And let our ordered lives confess
The beauty of thy peace.

Strivings, strain and stress
All too readily rule my frame;
The petty worries of every day,
Work and years sometimes seem
To press upon my brain.
While deep inside my inner pit,
Inadequacy and anxiety
Howl like hounds
Whose appetites feed on fret,
And yet,
The instruments of thy peace
Are all around me;
Not a feast of exquisite song
From a bird on a lonely heath,
But instruments more mundane
Like photographs and smiles
And cups of tea and the leaves
Of busy lizzies in plastic flower pots.

Your song sings in the sound of water
Running from a tap,
From down at heel pigeons
Cooing in the eaves,
Kettles boiling, winds whistling
Or waves breaking endlessly on a beach;
These are friends,
These laughing, talking, smiling
Instruments of thy peace.

There are friends
I never speak to
Because they live
In books and plays.
Performers on the television
Who in their myriad ways speak to me.
They are not the least
Of the instruments of thy peace.

Love surrounds me most in people,
Like those friends who are the healers, comforters,
The laughter makers who walk into my life,
Through my office, or through my kitchen door.
But those I love most
Who give me most
Are so very close that I am apt to ignore,
To miss, the kiss of peace they bring.
Yet when I emerge from under my shell
I am lifted, helped, dazzled by the love
Which is the wonder of the music
Of the instrument of peace.

Lord, I want to be
An instrument of your peace.
I sometimes wish I could do
Heroic things; be a saint;
Do something beautiful for you.
But there is nothing extraordinary about me.
I gaze at the great saints with awe
And their very saintliness is frightening.

Yet in my own experience
The instruments of your peace
Have never been very dramatic.
Your peace has come to me
Through simple, common things,
Acts of kindness,
Gestures of love from people
Who have accidentally given me a glimpse
Of your love.
But perhaps I can only bear to see a glimpse
Of the love that embraces the world,
The love that laughs, weeps, lives and dies
With and for the whole of humanity.
Perhaps a glimpse is all I can take.

Lord, let me reflect the light
That *is* given to me,
Let me recognise the love and the joy
And the peace that *is* in my life
And to share it,
With whoever will receive it.

Help me to be an instrument of your peace
In the very ordinary acts of my day,
From my rising to my sleeping,
In talking, in listening, in patience,
In caring, in laughing, in thinking.

Lord make me an instrument of thy peace,
Where there is hatred let me sow love;
Where there is injury, pardon;
Where there is discord, union;
Where there is doubt, faith;
Where there is despair, hope;
Where there is darkness, light;
Where there is sadness, joy;
For thy mercy's sake.
Amen.

THE LANGUAGE OF PRAYER

To explore the depths of human love takes a long time, a lifetime, or longer. To search the mystery of divine love takes eternity and that, poets say, is far too short. Left to my own devices I would have wasted so much time. Years and years could have been spent in a spiritual wilderness if it hadn't been for one thing, one thing that was right out of my control.

In infancy, before I could speak, I heard a particular language. As water was sprinkled on my head, I was received into the family of Christ. The precious sign of the cross was traced on my brow. Before I could speak, I was asked to walk with God all the days of my life. As others answered for me I heard the language of love, without understanding I heard my parents pray.

As I learned to speak, so I learned prayers, prayers that would never leave me. I didn't consciously learn them, I just heard them so often that I knew them; the Lord's Prayer, Glory Be To God, Hail Mary. I did memorise the mysteries of the rosary and learn the prayers of the mass because I wanted to be involved in the drama and mystery of candles and incense. I sang 'Kyries', listened with awe to the whispered words, 'Hoc est corpus meum', 'this is my body'; attended 'Benediction' and 'Holy Hour' services; was confirmed, made my first confession and communion; followed the stations of the cross; made 'Novenas' and grew into a scuffed-shoed, cut-kneed, scruffy lad who had heard the language of prayer, but through a glass, very darkly.

In those days prayer came as naturally as breathing. In retrospect they were happy days, mostly. Of course at the time they seemed to be full of the disasters and pains of growing up, but God was as real as my parents and my brothers. He was one of the family, unquestioned.

I used to play in a parish band in which my family were well represented, my father, my uncle and my cousins amounting to two trombones, two cornets and a tenor horn. It's odd, but there is a particular piece of music, 'Panis Angelicus', which whenever I hear it, I see my uncle with his trombone and the memory of the quality of those days comes flooding back.

Slowly, as it does for most of us, childhood began to disappear, and with it the ease of natural prayer. Questions began to push prayer into the background and soon the questions became all important.

I remember plucking up the courage to visit a priest, to present my questions to him. They worried me, these questions, I probably thought that nobody had ever asked them before. They were questions about the church.

I was playing my first semantic game of 'what does the church mean when she says . . .?' and out came the questions about the real presence, transubstantiation, Aristotle's theories about accidents and substance. I thought I was no end of a budding theologian. I remember the priest listening patiently, and then saying in his gentle Irish brogue, 'you know, the trouble with you is pride, intellectual pride, it's the devil making you ask these questions, the devil in the form of intellectual pride'. So I said to the priest, 'well, if it is the devil asking these questions, what do you say to the devil?' The priest smiled and said, 'get thee behind me Satan'.

I went off in a dissatisfied huff, but of course he was right, it was pride that was separating me from God. It took me a long time to realise that truth. It was very much later that I realised that I had fallen out with particular teachings of the church, but had never asked the basic questions, such as, 'Do I believe in God? Do I believe in Jesus?' Sadly I slid into a cynical agnosticism which lasted for several years.

I remember feeling slightly ashamed as a teenager in the forces abroad, in a moment of stress and fear I found myself saying 'Hail Mary . . .' I felt ashamed because I had let my principles go and resorted to prayer through fear. I also felt ashamed that when I

233

tried to pray the only words that I could form were those I had learned as a child, and in this situation they were not particularly appropriate. I felt ashamed because I didn't know how else to pray. It took several more years before I could turn to God and say simply, 'I don't know how to pray, but please come into my life, somehow'.

In time and through various experiences, I began to realise, that I had turned my back on God, but he had never left me. He was still as close as he was when I was a child. I wanted to start again, but it's not simple. The easy, natural acceptance had gone with childhood and innocence. The old priest was right, my intellect kept getting in the way, pride and doubt had become part of me.

It was at the least expected moment that I realised the presence of God. In the middle of an argument, when my cynicism was working at its hardest. Suddenly all the clever words, the doubts, just dropped away, like someone opening a curtain, for a brief moment, the arguments fell away before what was to me a moment of reality.

Since then I have discovered that there is no one way of praying. I have talked with God using the beautiful ancient prayers of the church, using my own stumbling words, and sometimes using no words.

Sometimes I hear a piece of music as a shout of praise. Sometimes I pray the news, just listen to the headlines and offer up the concerns of the day, the world. Sometimes I let the world shut God out again and it is a struggle to realise his presence. I find silence is often the best way back. The silence of a church, or inner silence that can be found sitting in a rush-hour train. Simply to sit quietly, not asking questions, not listing my problems, not saying anything, simply being still in his presence. It is in these moments when God lifts the curtain to reveal that most of the perils, changes and fears of my life come from within.

I sometimes go into retreat, perhaps for a week in some quiet house. I also go into retreat for much shorter periods. By that I mean, not weeks or days or hours, but seconds. In the middle of an ordinary day, I will close my eyes for a few seconds and in those seconds retreat to a place where I have known both the peace and the presence of God. Anyone can do it. We all know of such places and in the twinkling of an eye we can be there. For me there is a particular bay of an island in the Hebrides, which has a rock which we christened 'Oyster-catcher Island'. I have only to close my eyes and I am there, breathing in the beauty and the calm of one of God's great works of art.

That crag of rock
Whose head stands proud where shell and tide
Have formed a face;
Granite jowled and limpet eyed,
That watches cloud and rain-filled sky
And hears the piercing, plaintive cry
Of gull and oyster-catcher.

That rock
The children climbed, shouting,
With breathless counting of the steps
By which they timed the speed of their ascent.
That rock
Heather crowned and bird bespattered,
Stands in seaweed daily drowned by flooding seas
That break about its feet.

And still it stands
Serene with ancient calm,
Aloof, impassive
Unmoved by tears, untouched by grief
Of those whose fretful years are far too brief
For this eternal stone.

That ageless rock
Calls in its silence across the noisy clamour
Of the city,
And the passing drama of men struggling
For a short-lived space of comfort or power
Or a transitory place in the sun of our
Particular day.

The warlords and the captains
Took sightings from this tor
And dropped their sails to anchor in its lee.
But now, children's cries and breaker's roar
Join the endless washing of the sea
Above the buried bones and swords
Of yesterday's strife.

That rock
That feels the lap of silken smooth serenity
Yet hears the scream
And roar of a tempest sea
In all its agony.
That rock
Seen between the mists of heather blue,
Seems to know the sorrow and elation
Of the mind in whose creation
The sculptured souls of men
Are washed in a sea of love
And gathered into eternity.

And though my feet
Tread city's stone
And ears are tuned to thousands teeming,
Yet mind and heart still stand alone
By sea and rock forever dreaming
Of that endless day.

If it takes eternity to search out the mystery of divine love, then I have a long way to go before I even begin to fathom the depths, but this far I have come. I know that if I can be still, in my head, even for a few seconds, he will enter my mind, bring light where there is darkness, replace anxiety with his peace. In such brief moments of stillness, I am a child again. In such brief moments, I am deep in prayer.

INDEX OF TITLES